Benchmarking for Competitive Advantage

Benchmarking for Competitive Advantage

TONY BENDELL,
LOUISE BOULTER and JOHN KELLY

FINANCIAL TIMES

PITMAN PUBLISHING

Pitman Publishing
128 Long Acre, London WC2E 9AN

A division of Longman Group Limited

Grateful acknowledgements are due to the BSI for permission to use the
Kitemark on the cover illustration. The Kitemark is a Registered Product
Certification Mark and for further details please contact BSI QA,
PO Box 375, Milton Keynes, MK14 6LC. Tel: 0908 220908.

First published in Great Britain 1993

British Library Cataloguing in Publication Data
A CIP catalogue record for this book can be obtained from the British Library

ISBN 0 273 60168 7 ✓

15 14 13 12 11 10 9 8 7

Phototypeset in Linotron Times Roman by
Northern Phototypesetting Co. Ltd, Bolton
Printed and bound in Great Britain by
Biddles Ltd, Guildford and King's Lynn

CONTENTS

Acknowledgements   vi

1   So what's so special about Benchmarking?   I

2   Total Quality Management, business processes and the need for
    external comparisons   13

3   The pre-history of Benchmarking   29

4   The Birth of Benchmarking – the Xerox approach   55

5   What it's all about – The Benchmarking process   62

6   Internal Benchmarking   88

7   External Benchmarking and how to do it   110

8   Benchmarking in the public sector   123

9   Benchmarking in other difficult areas – R & D, Design
    and the Creative Service Sector   136

10 Relationship to International Awards criteria   159

11 Fighting your way through the hype – some simple 'do's' and
    'don'ts'   195

12 Summary of Benchmarking approaches and experiences   212

13 The future of Benchmarking   244

14 Assessing your starting point and building an Action Plan   247

Index   264

ACKNOWLEDGEMENTS

The authors would like to express their gratitude to all of the people and organisations who have contributed to this book.

We would like to acknowledge, in particular, the high level of co-operation, helpfulness, time and effort shown by the following individuals and organisations.

Chas McCann, Director of Business Quality and Technical Support, Rank Xerox, Hertfordshire for checking the draft of Chapter 4, Ray S. Robertson, manager, Operations Programme Management of NCR (Manufacturing) Limited in Dundee, for case study material in Chapter 5 and Mike James-Moore, manager, Manufacturing Strategy, Rover Group Ltd, Coventry for providing relevant material for the case study on the Rover Group also in Chapter 5; Tim Hurdle, staff relations manager, BOC UK Gases, Guildford, Surrey, for providing relevant material for the case study in Chapter 6; the International Benchmarking Clearinghouse, A Service of the American Productivity and Quality Centre for providing material on the Benchmarking Awards in the US in Chapter 10 as well as providing material for Chapter 11, the Benchmarking Code of Conduct; DTI for allowing us to use Figure 11.2, 'Troubleshooting', which can be found in the booklet 'Best Practice Benchmarking' available from the DTI and E.F.Q.M. for material from the brochure 'Total Quality Management, The European Model for Self-Appraisal 1993 (© E.F.Q.M. 1992 All rights reserved).[1] Finally a special thanks for all the employees of those organisations for the time, effort and patience which went into their contributions for Chapter 12, namely: D. G. Smith OfD Operations Manager, ICL in Berkshire[2]; Stephen Waldron, General Manager BOC Ltd, Surrey; Mike James-Moore, manager, Manufacturing Strategy, Rover Group Ltd, Coventry; Barry Povey, quality consultant, IBM Havant, Hampshire; Steve Jerman, Product Analyst product marketing, Computer Peripherals, Hewlett-Packard, Bristol; John Smith, Group Customer Relations Manager, Group Customer Relations Department, Abbey National, Milton Keynes; and Ian Ferguson, head of personnel services, British Gas PLC, London.

1 Further information regarding the European Quality Award and self-appraisal based on the Award Model can be obtained from E.F.Q.M., Brussels, Tel: 32 2 7753511, Fax: 32 2 7791237.
2 The article is ICL copyright, the whole or part of the article may not be reproduced in any form or by any means, electronic, photocopying, or otherwise without the written permission of the author, D. G. Smith.

1 SO WHAT'S SO SPECIAL ABOUT BENCHMARKING?

INTRODUCTION

It seems that Benchmarking has become a vogue phrase of the 1990s, but should it be? Is it just another management fad? The latest fashion? Or does it represent both an evolution and a revolution in business thinking? Undoubtedly, the answers to these questions are of some importance to the reader and, indeed, to all Western management.

The difficulty of these questions is not made easier by the confusion and mysticism surrounding Benchmarking. What is this magic new approach? How does it differ from what we have always been doing? How did it help Rank Xerox break through? What exactly do we need to do? How do we start and who can help us? Benchmarking means different things to different people. Naturally, some interpretations are more plausible than others.

It has been said that in the early 1990s it is almost impossible to read a management magazine or attend a management conference without some reference to Benchmarking. Magazine articles, conferences and training programmes are exploding in the United States and to some extent a similar Benchmarking tidal wave is under way in Europe.

A survey conducted in late 1991 among small, medium and very large US firms revealed that, compared with one year previously, more than 75 per cent of the survey sample believed that the amount of Benchmarking in their firms had increased. During the next five years, 96 per cent of these organisations expect still more Benchmarking. It is interesting that the same survey revealed that 79 per cent of respondents felt that companies will have to have Benchmarking to survive but that 95 per cent felt that most companies do not know how to Benchmark. Only 28 per cent thought it was a fad.

Further results indicate that leading companies from most industries are Benchmarking and that Benchmarking is not limited to any one type of industry. The majority of firms also consider themselves to be beginner or novice users of the Benchmarking process. Perhaps most interestingly, nearly half of the companies have been conducting Benchmarking studies for less than two years, while only 20 per cent have been Benchmarking for more than five years.

The 'Benchmarking Boom' has led to an ever-increasing level of requests from companies for co-operation and Benchmarking partnerships with others. Interestingly, the survey revealed that, despite this, 82 per cent of the companies sampled still do not have a formal process for responding to such requests.

In the UK, things are not much different. A recent survey of the top 1,000 companies by the Confederation of British Industry (CBI) and Coopers & Lybrand revealed that more than two-thirds of the 105 respondents from the manufacturing, service and other sectors claim to be Benchmarking, with 82 per cent of these regarding it as successful. Sixty-eight per cent intended to increase investment in Benchmarking in the next five years.

Why is this Benchmarking Boom happening? Is it structural or will it go away? Various commentators have pointed out that Benchmarking is a natural evolution of concepts of competitor and market analysis, quality improvement programmes, performance measurement and, perhaps most of all, Japanese practices. Its origins may, in one sense, be traced to the early primitive taking apart of products of competitors to see how they were made and how they could be made, whether the same or better.

This early physical Benchmarking progressed one step further when beginning in the late 1950s, the Japanese visited many thousands of companies around the world, mainly in America and Western Europe, specifically to absorb ideas that they could adopt, adapt and improve upon throughout manufacturing processes. They investigated Western products and processes to understand their good and bad features, and then built superior alternatives at a lower cost. They also transferred good practices and technology used in one business area to a completely different area, driven by commitment to company-wide continuous improvement.

When the Xerox Corporation in America adopted a similar vigorous approach in 1979, motivated by a rapidly diminishing market share, the birth of Benchmarking as we know it today had taken place. Xerox felt they had no choice. Their competitors were able to sell products more cheaply than Xerox could make them. To understand why this was, the product features and performance capabilities of competitive machines were rigorously evaluated and Xerox was also able to investigate the practices of Fuji Xerox in Japan. The improvement opportunities that were identified and put into place resulted in a swift turnaround for Xerox's fortunes and led to Best Practice Benchmarking becoming a central part of their business strategy. Today, Xerox and Rank Xerox Limited in the UK are generally recognised as the leaders in the Benchmarking field in the Western hemisphere.

The lead given by Xerox established the technique in America and it has become a qualifying condition for companies aiming for the prestigious Malcolm Baldrige Award for Quality. More recently it has become a criterion in the European Quality Award.

C. Jackson Grayson Junior, Chairman of the International Benchmarking Clearing House in the United States summarises the three principal drivers for the Benchmarking Boom as follows.

1 **Global Competition**   As the world becomes smaller, front-edge companies are realising that they must match or exceed best practices from competitors anywhere in the world in order to survive.

2 **Quality Awards** Increasing interest in the Malcolm Baldrige Award in the US and the new European Quality Award is fuelling the movement towards Benchmarking. As an indication the US Malcolm Baldrige Quality Award requires applicants to demonstrate competitive analysis and Benchmarking in 510 of the 1,000 points.

3 **Breakthrough Improvements**   There is increasing management awareness of just how far companies may be behind global competitors. After many years of having it good, they are only just now getting sensitised to the size of the gap. There is a growing realisation says Grayson, that small continuous improvements are not going to be sufficient. Often there are temporal differences between the best and the average in terms of quality time and product development, as well as cost gaps of perhaps 30 to 50 per cent. Most firms therefore, he argues, must obtain large improvements – breakthroughs just to catch up. They are learning from others, he says, that quantum changes are more likely to come from Benchmarking than from anything else.

Without doubt, a major reason for the current interest in Benchmarking is a natural evolution from Total Quality Management. Total Quality Management programmes have helped us to focus on what we are doing badly and how we can do it better. We set ourselves targets for improvement, continuous incremental improvement. However, unless we raise our eyes from the job in hand to look at what others are achieving and how they are achieving it, we may never realise that it is our business processes themselves, and not just their marginal inefficiencies, which are holding us back. The only way that we can drive our organisations to excellence is to ensure that we keep our eyes on our competitors and world's best practice in all aspects of the business. We must Benchmark performance and our internal processes by external comparisons against those better than us in order to drive us to improve and show us how to improve.

THIS BOOK AND THE MEANING OF BENCHMARKING

This book, then, is about Benchmarking: but what do we mean by that? Today, quite clearly, the term is ambiguous, woolly, a mystery. It appears to require great subtlety of understanding and clearly means different things to different people. Company practices vary dramatically in terms of their implementation or tentative enquiries in relation to Benchmarking. Some companies look for consortia of partners to, in some sense, get together and exchange information. Others look for rather broad, perhaps superficial, visits to world-leading or comparable companies to get a soft 'feel' for their way of doing things. Others employ consultants, who interpret Benchmarking as the collection and comparison of global, primarily financial, measures of company performance. This is often with similar companies in the same industry worldwide, or perhaps, those in comparable circumstances.

Not surprisingly, the lack of clarity about the meaning of Benchmarking has provided a field day for consultants who 'solve it all'. However, a consultant's report which shows poor financial performance, customer satisfaction or other high level attributes, in comparison to the performance of competitors, does not in itself assist the organisation to improve fundamentally. At this global, somewhat nebulous level, much of the problems of organisation are well known to the people in and managing them. These measures are fundamentally of output performance, they show how much or how little is being achieved by the organisation in comparison to competitors and to world's best practice. They do *not* show the weaknesses in the internal business processes or the strengths. They do *not* show how the competitors and world leaders are achieving what they are. They do *not* show what, if anything, is transferable to the organisation's particular circumstance and how to make that transfer. They do *not* in themselves, provide the degree of certainty that management needs in order to make the step change necessary in their behaviour or style. They do *not* provide the understanding of the 'why' that can only be achieved by the process of personal discovery.

Benchmarking on global measures by external consultants does not, and cannot, in itself provide a fundamental insight and change of practice that is necessary to transform the organisation from a potential world loser to a world winner. Nor can naïve, unstructured, unplanned, uninformed and often isolated attempts at Benchmarking by individuals within the organisation which is in itself not committed to and has not planned what it wants to do with Benchmarking. The attractive 'jolly' of visiting another company, particularly somewhere exotic, may be a perk of the job, but such visits are more likely to lead to a petering out of the interest in Benchmarking, or even bring it into disrepute, when they fail to deliver anything substantial.

The real role of Benchmarking has to be seen in the context of the organisation that is continuously looking at itself, analysing its performance and internal processes, and continuously implementing improvement. Modern management jargon might call this a Total Quality Management (TQM) organisation, but the jargon in itself is not important. Such an organisation is looking continuously to improve and planning improvement. In doing this, it will set itself targets and, for most organisations early in the improvement process, it is most likely that these targets will be improvements relative to its current performance. Often, a crucial first step is to identify both what are the key measures of current performance and actually how good we currently are. Once this is done, targets are established for improvement against time and an Action Plan put in place to achieve this. There is still, however, one thing missing. If the improvement targets are established in isolation of any knowledge of what others are doing and of what others are achieving, the targets may not be taxing enough to help our company or other organisation stay in business.

This book's view of Benchmarking, then, is not just about the comparison of measures, as it has often been mistaken to be. It is, instead, a natural development of the desire to improve and the process of improvement. As well as looking internally, one looks for ideas to 'borrow' or 'steal' from those that are doing better, even perhaps in one very specific aspect. In this sense, it is very much an integral part of the improvement process. Nor does the Benchmarking process stop when comparisons have been made and you have been found to be doing well or been found wanting. This is the first step; 'how' and 'why' need to be established, and methods of achivement evaluated for potential transfer, improvement upon and implementation. Implementation itself is part of the process.

This concept of Benchmarking, like TQM, has as one of its central ingredients, the concept of the internal business process. The crucial internal processes of the business need to be identified, and measures and measurement points have to be established. Comparisons in processes and process performance have to be made externally, as well as internally, and process improvements or redesign need to put in place. Instead of global Benchmarking measures, loved by some consultants, process Benchmarking becomes the key to improvement.

In this book, we consider the nature of the TQM revolution and the intrinsic importance of business processes. We look at where the TQM revolution falls short and at the need for external comparisons. We look at the pre-history of

Benchmarking from the various Quality Gurus, through the history of measurement and we come to the Xerox story; the story of Benchmarking for survival. We look at what Benchmarking is, and study separately the great benefits to be obtained by the planned use of internal and external Benchmarking within our organisations.

Public Sector Benchmarking has not received much attention in management literature to date, despite the great potential for process and service improvement that is available. We investigate this and also consider the application of Benchmarking in some of the more difficult areas; such as research and development, design, management and the creative service sector. The book also deals with the relationship to international award criteria such as for the Malcolm Baldrige Award, the Deming Prize and the European Quality Award. Finally, the book gives the reader some simple 'do's' and 'dont's' to fight your way through the hype, to help you start the process of implementing Benchmarking within your own organisation. To help you do this, we provide some simple self-examination forms for you to assess your starting point and build an action plan.

ISO 9000/BS 5750 AND BENCHMARKING

Given Benchmarking's origins in the US and ISO 9000's passage to world dominance developing from the UK, it perhaps is not surprising that the potential between these apparently dissimilar concepts has to date not been identified in the business literature. On reflection, however, such association may have advantages. For many organisations on the world scene, particularly medium sized and larger organisations who are more likely to have an interest in Benchmarking, there is a need, not an interest in obtaining certification to ISO 9000. This is a primary requirement that must be put in place to protect their market.

The spread of BS 5750 within the UK, its adoption as a European standard (EN 29000) and as an international standard (ISO 9000) may truly be said to be unprecedented. ISO 9000 is the international standard for Quality Systems, which provides a basis for assessing your organisation, or part thereof, against objective requirements of organisational discipline and control, traceability and the like. The standard requires that management show, define and document its policy and objectives for, and its commitment to, Quality.

Management is responsible for ensuring that the policies are understood, implemented and maintained at all levels of the organisation. Responsibility and authority throughout the organisation also must be defined, as well as the interrelationship of all personnel involved who manage, perform and verify work affecting Quality. In-house verification requirements must be identified, and adequate resources and trained personnel must be assigned for verification activities. A management representative for Quality must be assigned who, irrespective of other duties, has defined authority and responsibility for ensuring that requirements of the International Standard are implemented and maintained.

The organisation must establish and maintain a documented Quality System. This must include the preparation and implementation of procedures and work instructions, and must be periodically reviewed by management. Another clause requires that the organisation establishes and maintains procedures for contract review. Procedures must be established and maintained to control and verify the design of the product or service, in order to ensure that it meets the specified requirements. Document control is required.

Purchased product has to conform to the specified requirements and the organisation must ensure that this takes place. Adequate purchasing data must be included on purchasing documents. Where appropriate, the organisation needs to establish and maintain procedures for identifying product from applicable drawings, specifications or other documents during all stages of production, delivery and installation.

Other clauses deal, for example, with process control, inspection and testing, inspection measuring and test equipment, the control of non-conforming product, corrective action and handling, storage, packaging and delivery. Yet more concern the keeping of quality records, the conduct of internal quality audits, the identification of training needs and the provision of training. Where appropriate, servicing or the use of statistical techniques are also covered.

ISO 9000 then, provides a basic requirement in terms of a degree of belief in the organisational integrity of the company. What is its relevance to Benchmarking?

To answer this question, one should consider a particular aspect of the worldwide 'Benchmarking Boom'; the need to structure what appears to be a nebulous subject has led to many people developing pro formas, or forms, to capture information from other organisations in a way which allows comparability. At the top level, Benchmarking Grids have been produced which attempt to define the essential features of any organisation against which comparison is made. Such grids are typically not for all organisations, but for ones within a particular area of activity. An example of this is the Benchmarking Grid being utilised by the 'TQM in Research and Development Study Group' of the Quality Methods Association.

There is a sense, of course, in which ISO 9000 may itself provide a Benchmarking Grid for comparison between organisations. Since the Standard categorises essential aspects of the organisation, requires documentation of these in a way which is consistent with the Standard and auditable and, to some extent, therefore implies direct comparability of information between organisations, the Standard or an augmented version could be used for this purpose. Indeed, it is not much further, to see the various international award criteria, particularly those clearly auditable like the Malcolm Baldrige Award and the European

Quality Award, in a similar way. The self-assessment approach of the European Quality Award makes this particularly plausible.

HOW TO START

Most authors seem to have very preconceived notions of why the reader wants to read their book, if indeed, as all authors hope, they really do! We hope that the reader's interest is to obtain a deep understanding of the nature of the Benchmarking process, including what is currently being done, whether it is relevant, and how it should really be used and implemented within a process view of the world, as an intrinisic aspect of a quality improvement programme. None the less, we are realistic that many of you readers will be rather impatient. You will flick through this book looking for the key messages, reading parts of plausible chapters to locate, in a few minutes, what has taken us many months of research and writing to present to you. While we all know that you can only gain a limited first comprehension of the subject by this approach, none the less in a world in which we learn by doing, we would not wish to discourage you from learning enough to get started in this way.

If you must do it this way, then we do wish you luck but ask you to be careful. Do *not* ignore Chapter II with its simple 'do's' and 'dont's'. *Do* build an action plan. Do *not* rush ahead and get started and plan afterwards. In researching this book we found many examples of companies who, naïvely, have done it that way. The better ones learnt from their disappointing experiences, but many gave up.

Perhaps most fundamental of all, Benchmarking should be a team-based activity, integrated with other quality improvement activities within the organisation and closely connected to the planning activities going on at the top. To understand the subject, one might explore and dabble in isolation without real top management support and only lip-service. Once, however, comprehension has been obtained, then to make any progress one needs real top management commitment. Here is an area where consultants can be of assistance, since people seldom hear the profit in their own land. Top management must be convinced, and a champion or champions must be found, in order for an organisation to take this subject seriously. In the process of convincing top management, of strategically building Benchmarking into the business plan and the future, as well as in the introduction of skills, the spreading of experiences from the mistakes of others and in the facilitation role, consultants can be a great help. But they should not do it for you. Benchmarking should be done by your organisation, for your organisation and in order to improve your organisation. The responsibility is yours.

2 TOTAL QUALITY MANAGEMENT, BUSINESS PROCESSES AND THE NEED FOR EXTERNAL COMPARISONS

THE MEANING OF 'QUALITY'

Even the most cursory glance at advertisements on television, in the Press or on advertisement hoardings demonstrates that quality has become the 'buzz word' of the 1990s. Furthermore, it has become a strategic issue with major companies putting great emphasis on the steps they have taken to improve the quality of their product or service. Leaving aside any marketing hype, the common meaning and importance of the word 'quality' has changed over the past 50 years. Indeed, according to Armand Feigenbaum, one of the three major American Quality Gurus who introduced modern concepts of quality to Japanese industry in the early 1950s, quality in the West has now become the single, most important force leading to organisational success, and company growth in national and international markets.

What, then, is quality? What does it mean, how has it evolved into Total Quality Management (TQM), that all-embracing improvement culture, and why have so many organisations floundered on the route to its achievement?

Quality is one of today's most misunderstood and often

abused words. The meaning of quality is very much dependent upon the context in which it is used, and the perception of the persons transmitting and receiving that message. Indeed, the word quality may often quite deliberately be used ambiguously.

This brings us to an initial dilemma – that of quality meaning different things to different people, from the performance of a specific product or service offered to the consumer, to the way the entire organisation is managed.

While the word is used regularly to describe products, and we see advertising for 'quality carpets', 'quality double glazing' and so on, it can and often does cause confusion, since individual perceptions of what quality is will vary. In particular, in organisations, there is a clear need to understand what quality is, since exhortations to 'make quality products' will be interpreted in different ways by different people.

The modern use of the word quality and its high profile originated after Japan's defeat at the end of the Second World War. It was the Americans who exported the basic concepts of quality control to Japan, and the work of Dr Edwards Deming and Dr Joseph Juran laid the foundations for the subsequent revolution in Quality in Japan. It is indeed sad, and with hindsight most regrettable, that these two Americans had to travel abroad in order to have their message heard and understood. However, in Europe and the US the post-war boom was at a height and had created a situation in which the consumer, who had long been starved of essential basic commodities, never mind luxuries, would buy most items offered for sale. It was a production-led market.

Inevitably, the post-war boom years when companies could 'make it and ship it out' came to an end. The markets became saturated and product or service differentiation became less marked. Meanwhile, the Japanese were learning all they could about Western industrialised processes including marketing, finance, and, of course, quality. It has been said that at that time young Japanese managers came over to the West and saw that we wrote books about quality, made films about quality and gave talks about quality. What they failed to grasp, of course, was that we never actually did any of it! Those of more mature years will remember that during the 1950s and early 1960s the Japanese were taken to task for copying many Western products. Consumer items from the Far East were, in many cases, indistinguishable from 'the real thing'. In the midst of their indignation at this turn of events, Western organisations failed to notice that the Japanese were now setting about improving the products, which they had started by copying. More importantly, by this means, they learned a process which was repeatable for the improvement of quality. Thus from the beginning, Quality Improvement and physical Benchmarking went hand in hand.

It could be said that the word quality is used so frequently nowadays that its real meaning has been lost to many people. Used in its traditional way, the word quality has often been used to denote excellence, beauty or high cost. This rather nebulous and imprecise concept, however, is of little use within most organisations. A useful definition of quality is meeting the requirements of the customer and a necessary first step is therefore to define those requirements. Typically the word 'requirements' has been equated with 'specification', often ignoring criteria of price or delivery, in addition to product characteristics, so that quality has often been defined as conformance to specification.

However, this particular approach does have several weaknesses. For example, it can over emphasise inspection which aims to ensure that nothing outside the specification is delivered to the consumer. This can lead to a rather 'hit and miss' type of operation where the only way of protecting the customer from defective products or poor service may be to put a great deal of emphasis on end-point inspection, which is unreliable anyway. An additional difficulty with this approach is that it takes place when the product or service is at its most expensive, that is, when all the work is complete. In addition, it is also the most critical time to ascertain whether the end product is good enough or not, because the next stage is delivery to the customer, and failure of product or service will usually mean failure to deliver. It is essential to realise that quality cannot be inspected in, but must be designed and manufactured into, the product or service. Increasing the end-line inspectors ten-fold will not improve the manufactured quality of the 'product'; it will just reduce the chances of the customer receiving defectives.

Not only are such inspection processes expensive and time-consuming, they can create a climate in which quality of the product for the customer is considered satisfactory because it passes inspection and therefore does not need to be improved. Furthermore, it does not take into account the changing requirements and needs of the customer, and the market place in which the organisation has to operate.

TOTAL QUALITY MANAGEMENT, CUSTOMERS AND MEASUREMENT

Early approaches to quality and, in particular, quality control and quality assurance, focused on the product. As the markets for products became saturated following the post-war boom years, suppliers began to realise that the customer was looking for a total service, not just the product, and therefore the need became apparent for departments such as marketing, design and accounting equally to identify and focus on the needs of customers. So it was that the concept of TQM, which embraced the whole organisation, came into being.

From the very early days Total Quality Management (TQM) has meant different things to different people. Some have treated it purely as a motivational campaign aiming to improve service to external customers. Others have focused on internal training as a way of motivating and giving people tools to undertake improvement activities. Many have identified that beyond training, teamwork and the use of statistical techniques there is, in TQM, the quest for the self-improving organisation. While cultural change, organisational change and the use of simple tools, together with a documented quality system, all have a part to play, TQM requires a refocus and redirection of the business, as depicted in Figure 2.1.

- Fundamental cultural shift from Quality Assurance, Quality Control
- Theme of Continuous Improvement
- Customer orientated (internal and external)
- 'Right first time' standard
- Everybody in the company involved
- Led by senior management
- Measure Quality Costs/Critical Success Factors
- Prevention philosophy
- Supported by Quality Management System

Figure 2.1   Basic principles of TQM

Some of the organisational issues that may be apparent in any organisation are shown in Figure 2.2. There are subtle deficiencies that go beyond conventional definitions of product or service Quality Assurance. Resolving these is what TQM is about. The purpose is to develop a self-improving organisation, that is one in which the rest position is improvement; one in which if you never did any else to the organisation again, it would carry on improving (Figure 2.3).

Total Quality Management is a strategic approach aimed at producing the best product or service currently available through innovation and continual improvement. It is recognising that each person within the organisation is – or should aim to be – the expert within their particular role or function, and it is that person who has, quite often, first-hand knowledge of the process and therefore ideas on how to improve it.

- No clear relationship with customers
- No awareness of cost of quality
- Suspect workforce are underutilised
- No real measurement of staff performance
- Need to understand the real purpose of the group
- No clear picture of total rework
- No description of output quality
- Redundant procedures need updating
- No standard operating model for the department
- Difficulty in identifying internal improvement areas

Figure 2.2   Possible Organisational Issues

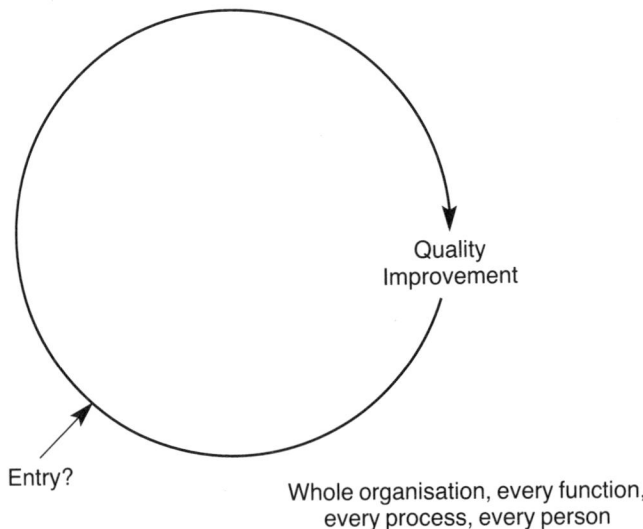

Quality
Improvement

Entry?

Whole organisation, every function,
every process, every person

Figure 2.3

In organisations that have treated TQM purely as a motivational campaign, we often see posters around the walls exhorting employees to 'Get it right first time'. While this objective is highly commendable, it can often appear as an insult to someone who has worked for a company for ten years, and has, as far as he or she is aware, been getting it right first time. The problem normally is that we have not all, by discussion, agreed what the 'it' is we are trying to get 'right first time'.

So, how did we start?

In theory it is simple – all we need to do is construct a plan, identify problems and opportunities for improvement, and systematically address them in priority order, reprioritising as the need arises.

In starting to execute this plan, different critical issues will be of different importance in various organisations. Those shown in Figure 2.4 correspond to a small manufacturing company – but frequently there is commonality in areas such as the need to clarify vision at top management level, communication problems and customer focus.

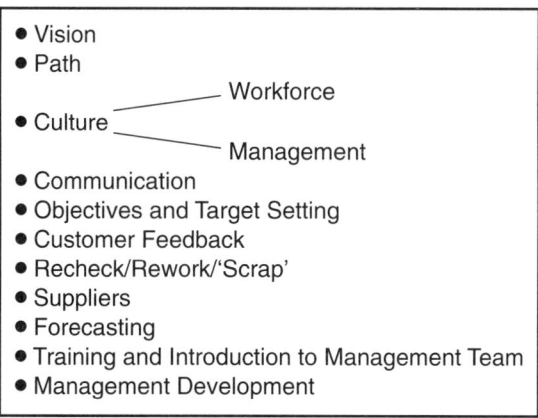

Figure 2.4   Critical Issues

There are essentially three stages to the path of TQM, as illustrated in Figure 2.5. A crucial stage, often neglected, is to start by finding out where you are now. In consequence it is recommended that at the start of TQM implementation the organisation undertakes initial data collection, including anonymous questionnaires and independent interviews with members of the workforce, as well as heads of function, in order to identify gaps in practices and procedures, inadequate

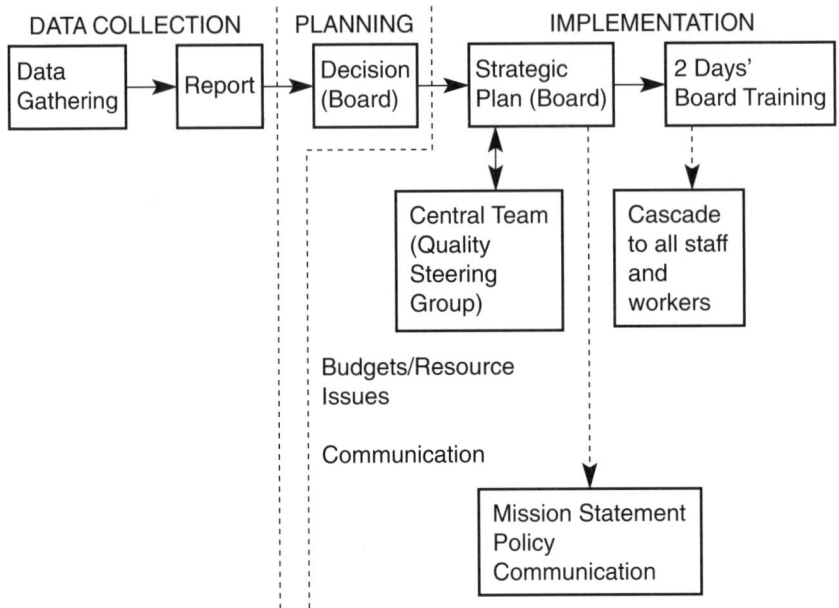

Figure 2.5

management, poor communication and problems encountered by people in doing their jobs.

A good way forward at the start of the implementation stage is for a small Quality Steering Group, preferably chaired by the Managing Director, to be established to manage the path to TQM. It will decide resources, monitor, facilitate and remove barriers to progress. Basic awareness training is now necessary and the board needs to commit itself long term by issuing a Mission Statement to tell the employees, customers, suppliers and possible other 'stakeholders' which is the path forward. Experience suggests that a 'cascade' model of training rather than 'wall-to-wall' training is to be preferred for TQM awareness.

It can be observed that many Mission Statements issued by organisations bear a striking resemblance to each other. This is not surprising, since after all there are only so many ways of saying more or less the same thing. Experience shows, however, that an organisation is missing the point if it merely copies another Mission Statement. It is the journey towards construct-ing the Mission Statement which is important, that is, the mental exercise for the Board of Directors of disagreeing, arguing and coming to a common conclusion about what the organisation is trying to achieve. Typically, the vision will be of increased profit, increased growth, greater creativity and innovation, and may well allude to the harnessing of the efforts of every person in the organisation towards their common aims. But how are these to be achieved? That answer is only by totally satisfying and indeed delighting the customer. While this might seem a self-evident truth, it is not unusual to see Mission Statements, Policy Statements or Quality Policies which totally ignore the customer.

Also, we need to specify what is it that we want project teams, quality circles or individuals to do; what we want them to achieve; it is for this reason that the Mission Statement or Quality Policy Statement is of vital importance.

Who is the customer?

It will be crucially important to the success of any organisation embarking upon a Total Quality Management initiative to understand what the end customer wants, and to define the needs and expectations of those customers clearly. However, to many people employed within the organisation, meeting the requirements of the customer can seem irrelevant. This is not surprising since perhaps only a very small percentage of all employees ever meet customers, never mind having meaningful face-to-face discussions with them, so how can they hope to understand and interpret their needs? Every person within an organisation, whether a secretary, an accounts clerk or an operator, has a role to play in improving quality for the end customer, but they often fail to realise this because they are distanced from that end customer.

It is helpful, therefore, if everybody within the organisation realises that they are themselves both an internal customer and an internal supplier. The internal customer is the next person or department in line to whom they supply work, information, decisions or resources. Similarly, they will have internal suppliers, that is, all those people who supply what is necessary for them to carry out their work. If, at any stage, there is a breakdown in these continuous customer/supplier relationships within the organisation, then the quality of the end product or service to the external customer will be less than satisfactory, as shown in Figure 2.6.

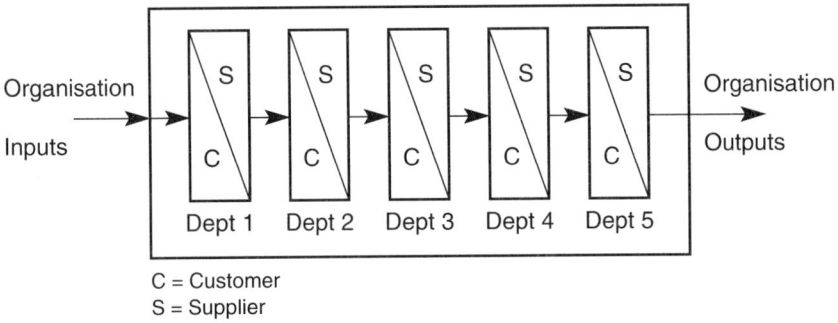

Figure 2.6   The customer/supplier chain

A key to improving the operations within the organisation is this concept of internal customers and suppliers. Each person is, or should be, *the* expert at their own job and will understand better than any one else the barriers which prevent them from doing the job better. This approach is the basis for project teams or, indeed, Quality Circles.

How are we progressing?

Establishing a Mission Statement for the organisation can have a salutory effect, particularly on senior managers and directors. Weeks of discussions and arguments, together with several iterations on the statement itself, can lead those involved to falsely conclude that they have now accomplished their task. Typically, the organisation will publicise its Mission Statement, particularly internally to all employees, who will read that the aim is to satisfy customers 'totally' or 'to become the best'. The Mission Statement, internally at least, will have very little value unless we explain to those who will be involved in the improvement process the role they have to play. The warehouse operator, the forklift driver and the secretary may well all ask (rightly?): 'So what do you want me to do?'

Likewise, in two years' time, how is the organisation to understand whether it has progressed or not, and whether there are barriers and obstacles still to be overcome? Unless we can measure how we are performing, at least internally, we will have no monitor of our progress towards the mission. At the very minimum, therefore, it is essential that, at all stages of Total Quality Management implementation, we make clear statements to everyone in the organisation about:

1 What we are aiming for;
2 Where we are now.

So, what should we measure?

Historically, measurement has typically concentrated upon outputs and inputs. Examples of this might be the weekly production figures, monthly profit, final scrap figures or costs. This information, while valuable, can come too late to significantly effect the processes to which they relate. This problem has been compounded in many organisations by the fact that measurement has concentrated almost exclusively on financial data. While the language of money is understood by most people, it does not entirely answer the question of how they should change what they do, in order to achieve better results. Perhaps even more importantly, it does not help them prioritise the key factors which are affecting their output results.

Clearly, some form of measurement is essential in order to monitor progress towards the stated aims. However, often in the past, measurement has been carried out for its own sake. This in turn has led to a plethora of measurements and measurement methods, particularly at the commencement of TQM initiatives, which are unfocused and therefore confusing to those involved. What is required is a unified measurement system which can be used for planning, for monitoring and for driving improvement. Ideally, the measurements used should indicate clearly how the organisation is progressing towards its mission, and should avoid the failures of the past in which most measurement was either financial and/or historic and so unfocused as to be confusing. The key to any successful measurement system is simplicity, both in the nature of individual measures and in the means by which it is unified into a coherent, focused whole.

Moreover, it must be recognised at the outset that many employees will have an inherent fear of measurement. This can possibly be traced back to previous unhappy experiences at the mercy of badly applied external measurement; measurement by those who did not carry out the process itself, but were paid to measure and control the performance of others. If we are to obtain accurate, reliable and meaningful measurement at the point at which it is crucial for control, it is essential that such fears are removed.

CRITICAL SUCCESS FACTORS AND BUSINESS PROCESSES

A unified approach to measurement can be obtained by identifying critical success factors. These represent a small number of key indicators that are such that if they are showing satisfactory progress towards targets, the organisation generally will be perceived as being successful on its path of quality improvement. The Critical Success Factors identified should be directly linked to the Mission Statement so that as a group these factors indicate progress, or otherwise, towards the mission of the organisation. This, again, sets a severe challenge for senior management, since the set of Critical Success Factors needs to be complete in order to convey the total picture. However, they must not be so extensive that they confuse the issues involved. Typically, Critical Success Factors may include measures of profit, cost, on-time delivery performance, sales and so forth. The organisation should seek to limit the number of Critical Success Factors to about 6 or 8, but certainly no more than 12.

Having established, then, the link between the Mission Statement and organisational performance by means of Critical Success Factors, each department and group of individuals can then identify the measurements that they can contribute to improving in order to help the organisational mission. In order to contribute to improvements in these Critical Success Factors, it will also be beneficial to identify key measurements on particular business processes.

What is a process?

Processes can be defined as mechanisms by which inputs are transformed into outputs. Outputs may well include a service, product, paperwork or materials, which differs from the original inputs. For example, the generation of a Purchase Order to a supplier may well involve several different stages or process steps. Each of these stages, typically, will belong to different personnel or different departments and no one person within the organisation is often responsible for the total process, other than the Managing Director. Historically, most organisations have been structured on a vertical, departmental or functional model. However, most processes within the organisation flow across the organisation, that is horizontally, passing from department to department or person to person. It is not surprising, therefore, that the external customer very often does not receive what was requested. We can liken many business processes to a relay race, with the baton passing from person to person within the organisation. As in a relay race in real life, the problems occur at the changeover points where the baton is dropped.

Identifying key business processes, the owners and the boundaries of each part of the process are key elements in the implementation of TQM. There are techniques available to assist with this identification, such as process deployment flowcharting, but these are not the subject of this book. In satisfying this requirement for the clarification and simplification of processes, documented quality management systems such as ISO 9000 may play a key role .

In order to monitor the progress of the organisation towards its goals, various types of business process measurement may be used. Effectiveness measures how good the output is from the process. One aspect of this is accuracy, i.e. is it correct or not, if so by how much? Reliability tells us how many times it is correct and timeliness indicates if it is late, and by how much. Volume is also important and efficiency tells us how well the resources are utilised.

While the above types of measurement are appropriate at the end of the process, it is far more important to use them at the end of each process stage, internally to the process itself. This will assist the organisation in ensuring early that the outcome to the ultimate customer is satisfactory. Process measurement can also provide feedback which gives an individual or a department the opportunity to improve while the work is being performed, so that they can correct the parameters within their control. Feeding back information in this way directly into the process enables two possible savings to be made:

1 Employees do not continue to make errors;
2 Resources are not added to an already effective system.

It is essential that process measurements are taken as close as possible to the source of any potential errors. Some measurements may be only taken for a short time, for example where a particular parameter or performance level is difficult to measure. This will ensure that disruption to process flow is minimised.

To identify a process then, we must look at the provision of product or service to a customer and the steps to provide it, we must ask how it is delivered and follow the workflow through the organisation, from first input stage. To describe a process, some sort of flowcharting is particularly useful or we can rely on procedure writing such as is common in Quality Assurance systems and implementing ISO 9000. To analyse processes, we can look at those flowcharts, at the exception paths and the boundaries, and all other aspects, in order to identify deficiencies. These may include 'holes' in the process when certain particular peculiar circumstances occur, unnecessary repetitive operations, clear organisational inefficiencies, inherent lack of customer contact, overcomplicated procedures of a bureaucratic nature and lack of ownership. We can also monitor and measure the processes with a view to an improvement in performance and customer satisfaction.

To put such measurement into place, the crucial thing is that we must have a clear consensus as to why it is necessary and how we are going to do it. Top management must be clearly and visibly behind it, and they must take the trouble to explain to the organisation what it is, why it is being implemented and how.

THE NEED FOR EXTERNAL COMPARISONS

Having analysed the business processes, and put in place key

measurements, the 'TQM organisation' will be carefully monitoring progress towards its stated goals. However, the question
arises as to whether the goals have been set realistically, yet in
an unbiased manner. Equally importantly, the *rate* of improvement will also be a crucial factor since, if competitors are
improving faster, then the organisation will be left behind.
Typically, as in the case of financial budgets for example,
targets may have been set on the basis of an internal view of
'better than last year'. This is somewhat akin to steering the ship
by looking out over the stern.

Today, for many businesses, competition is on the world
stage and, in the critical areas selected, the only sensible goals
are 'world best practice'. For many other companies,
competing in smaller arenas, the targets may not always be as
stringent, but the need for realistic goal-setting is just as important. Benchmarking is a method for making sure that the targets
aimed for are relevant to market demands and not arbitrarily
established by a finger in the air or extrapolation from last
year's achievements. The technique is equally applicable in
manufacturing and service organisations, and in the public and
private sectors.

Making comparisons with competitors is not a new idea.
Acquiring data about how one's competitors are performing,
what their product range comprises, what prices they are able to
command, and perhaps their operating methods, has always
been part of the marketing function's *modus operandi*.
Benchmarking today, however, is much more sophisticated
than a furtive, mainly reactive, short-term data-gathering
exercise. Instead, it is a highly-respected proactive management tool which is increasingly being used to identify and focus
improvement activities with the goal of international
competitiveness. The Japanese, perhaps, made it into an art
form and Xerox gave it a Western name.

3 THE PRE-HISTORY OF BENCHMARKING

WHERE DOES BENCHMARKING COME FROM?

Throughout history, people have developed methods and tools for setting, maintaining and improving standards of performance. One can trace the desire to improve performance and the actual process of improvement as far back as the early civilisations; from the ancient Egyptians who developed accurate methods of measurement by the use of a tool, referred to as the 'royal cubit', to the ancient Greeks who left us with exemplars of architecture, art and design, to the Romans who built upon the achievements of both the Egyptians and Greeks by developing the ability to construct bridges and roads to standardised designs.

In order to understand the evolutionary development of Benchmarking, in this chapter we put it into context of earlier Quality themes; from the early development of standards in relation to the control of Quality, the development of Statistical Process Control, the emergence of the Quality Gurus and Total Quality Management, to the early approach by the Japanese to Benchmarking. In a very real sense, Benchmarking is a natural evolution from principles of Quality Measurement and Total Quality Management (TQM); the natural next step in a story that began before the Industrial Revolution.

THE EARLY DEVELOPMENT OF STANDARDS FOR THE CONTROL OF QUALITY

During the early part of the Middle Ages, associations were established by master craftsmen. They were not only established to enhance and protect their members' livelihoods, but also for the maintenance of standards in relation to quality. This was taken a stage further by the introduction of the Guild Act of England which appointed 'wardens' to ensure that work was of a certain acceptable level. Both of these controls were an early means of quality control in relation to the products being produced.

Towards the middle of the eighteenth century there was a shift in emphasis in relation to the type of work which was being carried out, with a move away from the work being produced by craftspeople and a move towards factory-based processes. The majority of the working population were consequently involved in the operation of machinery, the advent of what we now identify as the Industrial Revolution.

During this period one can point to people's desire to improve performance and maintain quality. This is exemplified by the inventor of the cotton gin (a machine used for mechanically extracting cotton fibre from seed pods), Eli Whitney (1765–1825), who applied mass production techniques to the manufacturing of 10,000 muskets for the US army. The creation of jigs/templates/moulds had the effect of ensuring that all manufacturing parts were identical and therefore interchangeable, which resulted in the whole of the assembly operation being speeded up, with Whitney undertaking an analysis of workloads to determine how many operators a supervisor could manage effectively.

Frederick Winslow Taylor (1856–1917), another American, developed Eli Whitney's production methods a stage further. Taylor developed a system now referred to as 'Scientific

Management' or 'Taylorism'. Stop-watches were given to foremen and jobs were broken into their component elements, times to achieve an optimum performance were recorded which then became work standards.

During this time, not only was the production process speeded up, but the maintenance of quality also became regulated. It is no surprise that, by the end of the nineteenth century, as a consequence of Taylorism, supervisors had more people reporting to them and, in order that supervisors could concentrate more on production issues, it became common for the quality to be checked by inspectors who had no direct involvement with, or responsibility for, the production process.

THE DEVELOPMENT OF STATISTICAL QUALITY CONTROL

The requirements for mass production were accelerated by the onset of the First World War. As a consequence, mass production brought with it more inspection in the production process. In response to this, the Technical Inspection Association was formed shortly after the war and was subsequently incorporated as the Institute of Engineering Inspection in 1922 and later became the Institute of Quality Assurance in 1972. Nevertheless, inspection is not a wholly reliable method of quality control and, not only is it time-consuming, it is also expensive in terms of person power.

A consequence was the development of Statistical Quality Control. In the 1920s in the US, Western Electric (telecommunication giants) established a Inspection Engineering Department at their Bell laboratories in New York. It was here that Dr Walter A. Shewhart, generally regarded as the originator of Statistical Quality Control, designed the first control charts, and applied statistical methods to the measurement and control of quality.

Shewart's control charts necessitated the application of quality measurement and quality control at the point of manufacture instead of at the end of the line. Instead of inspection being carried out at the end of the line, critical steps in a process were sampled regularly, measurements taken and recorded chronologically on control charts. Various chart interpretation rules have been developed which allow the process operator to establish whether or not the process is in statistical control or not. Where there is non-conformance of a product the process can be stopped and the cause of the 'out of control' condition may be investigated and remedied before resuming production. Any excessive incidence of non-conforming product is consequently prevented during the process, instead of being appraised at the end of the process. The advantages of this are numerous, since there is a reduction in non-conforming product, as well as a saving in costs.

Shewart's methodology can also bring about additional improvements in quality. Shewhart stressed that there was a difference between 'common' causes of variation and 'special' or 'assignable' causes of variation. 'Common' causes of variation may be defined as being part of the system and beyond the operator's control, while 'assignable' causes of variation may be assigned to specific circumstances. The initial work of setting up the control charts necessitates the removal of as many of the special causes as possible, so that the process runs in statistical control, demonstrating only common causes of variation. Additional special causes may present themselves for removal, and also management can take steps to remove some of the common causes and thus improve the overall variability of the process.

In 1925, one of Shewart's colleagues, Harold E Dodge, developed statistically-based methods of acceptance sampling: methods which allow the user to get an accurate appreciation of the quality of a consignment by inspecting and measuring only a part of it.

THE SECOND WORLD WAR AND THE EMERGENCE OF THE QUALITY GURUS

The Second World War was responsible for the establishment of statistical techniques of measuring, evaluating and controlling quality, both in the US and in the UK. From this, the principles of quality management were established, and is what we now know today as Total Quality Management (TQM). TQM is now recognised as being one of the tools which has been such a driving force in the establishment of the Japanese as International exporters.

Since the Second World War various 'Quality Gurus' have made significant contributions to our Quality methodology and thinking. These are individuals who have led to the development of what we now call TQM and its caveat, Benchmarking.

The Quality Gurus discussed in this chapter are Deming, Juran, Feigenbaum, the American Gurus who visited Japan shortly after the Second World War; and Ishikawa, Taguchi and Shingo, the Japanese Gurus. All of these Gurus have made significant contributions in the field of quality improvement.

Dr W. Edwards Deming

Edwards Deming was born in 1900, in Iowa, USA, and was awarded his Ph.D. in mathematical physics from Yale in 1928. He joined the US Department of Agriculture and in 1936 he came to England to study for a time under Fisher.

Deming had met Shewhart in 1927 and worked closely with him thereafter. Whereas Shewhart had concentrated on manufacturing processes, Deming believed that the same concepts could be applied in other areas. In 1939, when Deming moved to the National Bureau of the Census, he applied Shewhart's statistical techniques to routine clerical operations. This resulted in some processes showing a six-fold productivity improvement, massive savings and the census report being published earlier than usual.

Attempts to meet the increased demands in materials for the war effort in America meant that many unskilled personnel were recruited by the manufacturing industries. Quality levels fell as a result and, in 1942, courses to teach various statistical approaches for the measurement and control of quality were quickly organised throughout the US, some 31,000 personnel undergoing training. Both Deming and Shewhart were active in this effort and Deming himself led 23 courses. His training in his own and Shewhart's methods, to designers, inspectors and engineers, resulted in substantial reductions in scrap and rework, together with productivity improvements. (Several people involved with this training programme banded together in 1946 to establish the American Society for Quality Control.)

The gains in the use of statistical techniques for quality control made during the war were short-lived, both here and in the US. In the boom market that developed, everything would sell, regardless of quality. Furthermore, many of the managers running the factories were not fully committed to the approach. To quote Deming from Nancy R. Mann's *The Keys to Excellence. The Story of the Deming Philosophy*, London, Mercury, 1989.

> The courses were well-received by engineers, but management paid no attention to them. Management did not understand that they had to get behind improvement of quality and carry out their obligations from the top down. Any instabilities can help to point out specific times or locations of local problems. Once these local problems are removed, there is a process that will continue until someone changes it. Changing the process is management's responsibility. And we failed to teach them that.

Shortly after the war, Deming went twice to Japan to assist

Japanese statisticians in studies of housing and nutrition, and for preparation of the census of 1951. It was during these visits that he met members of JUSE, the Union of Japanese Scientists and Engineers, which had been founded in 1946 to aid the rebuilding of Japan. A delegation from Bell Telephone Laboratories also visited Japan at about this time to demonstrate how the statistical methods, as developed and taught by Shewhart and Deming, could be used for controlling and improving quality in the Japanese telecommunications industry. Deming was invited to Japan again, this time by JUSE.

The Japanese were aware of British Standard 6000 and also the Z-I American Standards developed during the war, but because the statistical approach was difficult to understand, it was not accepted widely. Ishikawa, in *'What is Total Quality Control? The Japanese Way'*, London, Prentice Hall, 1985, wrote.

> In management, Japan also lagged behind, using the so-called Taylor method in certain quarters . . . Quality control was totally dependent on inspection, and not every product was sufficiently inspected. In those days Japan was still competing with cost and price but not with quality. It was literally still the age of 'cheap and poor' products.

Deming returned to Japan in June 1950 and taught over 500 managers and engineers about the importance of understanding an controlling variation, and the use of control charts, in a series of eight-day courses. He also introduced a systematic approach to problem solving and improvement, known variously as the Shewhart cycle (by Deming himself), the Deming cycle and the PDCA cycle.

This Plan, Do, Check, Action cycle shown in Figure 3.1, is an improvement methodology involving a feedback loop. The normal tendency, without the discipline imposed by the cycle, is to skimp on the planning and checking phases (target setting

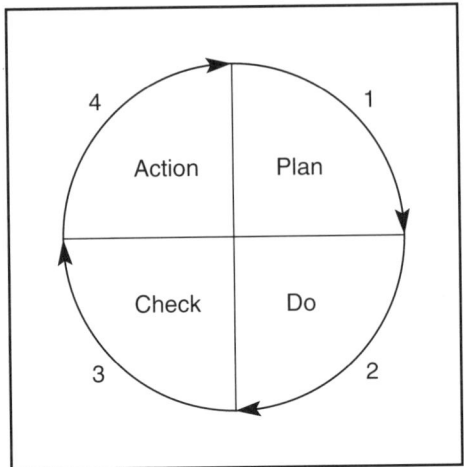

Figure 3.1   The PDCA (Plan, Do, Check, Action) Cycle

and monitoring), and perhaps to concentrate on the doing element. This leads to re-acting or fire-fighting, instead of a controlled assessment of the situation and then further action based on fact. It has been suggested that this may be because of the results-orientated society we live in, where doing is seen as being productive (and is easily measurable) and planning may be seen as procrastination.

Deming was determined to avoid a repetition of the situation that he had seen develop in America after the war. He made arrangements through JUSE to address senior managers to make them aware of the roles and responsibilities that they must take on board if Japanese industry was to turn itself around by making improvements in its quality performance, so that they could compete internationally. He stressed the need for working closely with suppliers to improve the uniformity and reliability of incoming materials, and also the need for maintenance of equipment.

He also emphasised the importance of the consumer and, in subsequent visits in 1951 and 1952, when he addressed many more engineers and top managers, he supplemented his usual courses with lessons on consumer research and modern methods of sampling. He taught that 'the consumer is the most important part of the production line' and his courses committed his students to carrying out door-to-door surveys in order to measure consumer requirements.

In the West, it was not until the 1970s that Deming started to make an impact. In 1980 when NBC, the American broadcasting company, made a documentary entitled '*If Japan Can, Why Can't We?*', many more became aware of his concepts. However, Deming is constantly reviewing and refining his ideas, and his more recent work is more management based than statistically based. His famous 14 points for management were produced to help people to understand and implement 'the total transformation of Western style of management' that he believes to be necessary. The 14 points, and more of Deming's recent thinking, are captured in his 1986 book, *Out of the Crisis*, Cambridge University Press, 1986.

Deming was awarded the Shewhart Medal by the American Society for Quality Control in 1956 and, in 1960, he became the first to be awarded the Second Order of the Sacred Treasure, the highest decoration that can be conferred on a non-Japanese. He was awarded the National Medal of Technology in America in 1987.

Dr Joseph M. Juran

Another recipient of the Second Order of the Sacred Treasure, though not until 1980, is Joseph Juran. Juran was born in Romania in 1904 and moved to America at an early age. He trained as an engineer, but his career has been varied; industrial executive, government administrator, university professor, labour arbitrator, corporate director and management consultant. He went to Japan in 1954, also at the invitation of JUSE.

With his broad experience in management, coupled with his

expertise in quality methods, he was able to discuss the wider issues of quality measurement and to appeal to senior Japanese managers. His lectures focused on planning and organisational issues, management's responsibility for quality, and the need to set goals and targets for improvement. He emphasised that quality control should be conducted as an integral part of management control. His lectures were followed up at more junior management levels by JUSE and the Japanese Standards Association. Large companies started internal training, courses for foremen were offered on national radio and booklets were made available at newspaper kiosks.

In the first edition of the *Quality Control Handbook*, J.M. Juran *et al*. (ed), New York, McGraw Hill, 1988, he coined the phrase 'There is gold in the mine'. This was a reference to the huge cost saving that can be made by measuring and resolving quality problems. However, it is not at the surface; you have to dig for it. Juran knew that making quality improvements is not easy; there are many barriers and obstacles to be overcome. Juran has used the measurement of costs attributable to quality problems within an organisation to capture the attention of senior management in the West.

Quality costs can also be used to prioritise and monitor improvement activity. Juran believes that at least 80 per cent of quality problems result from the systems and procedures laid down by management, so exhortations to the workforce to try harder will only serve to alienate them. Instead, he advocates the use of cross-functional management teams for achieving quality improvement. He teaches a project-by-project approach to solving quality problems and was probably the first to recommend the use of the Pareto principle for prioritising actions; identifying and tackling the 'vital few' problems and not the 'useful many'.

Juran also stresses the need for planning for quality. He sees quality planning as part of the quality trilogy of quality planning, quality control and quality improvement.

Quality control is the responsibility of the operating personnel, maintaining the status quo by following procedures, monitoring outputs and fire-fighting if necessary. Quality improvement has already been discussed, and it concerns the measurement and reduction of what Juran calls chronic quality problems.

Quality planning uses the lessons learned while making improvements to ensure that similar problems are avoided in the future. In *Juran on Planning for Quality*, J.M. Juran, New York, The Free Press, 1988, the key elements in implementing company-wide strategic quality planning are seen as identifying customers and their needs; establishing optimal quality goals; creating measurements of quality; planning processes capable of meeting quality goals under operating conditions; and producing continuing results in improved market share, premium prices, and a reduction of error rates in the office and factory.

Each stage of the planning process has inputs and outputs. Throughout the process there is a series of suppliers (of the inputs) and customers (for the outputs). Juran sees these supplier–customer relationships extending beyond the planning phase and on through all the steps involved in actually supplying the goods or service to the end user or consumer. The public in general may be regarded as a customer if the product or service (or the provision of it) impacts sufficiently on it.

Measurement must be introduced throughout this supplier–customer chain to evaluate, control and improve what the customer (internal or external) receives. The type, frequency and method of measurement will depend on the stage of the process and the people who will use it.

Juran, like Deming, has been critical of senior management in the West, but he sees the 1990s as the time when the improvement efforts made by Western organisations over the last decade will finally bear fruit.

Dr Armand V. Feigenbaum

Armand Feigenbaum was the third major American quality expert to visit Japan in the 1950s. Now 72, he is somewhat younger than the two previous gurus. In the 1950s, as Head of Quality at the General Electric Company, he had extensive contacts with Japanese companies such as Toshiba and Hitachi, and his 1951 book has been translated into Japanese.

Feigenbaum argued for the involvement of all functions within the quality process, not just the manufacturing area. The idea is to build quality in at an early stage instead of relying on process control and inspection further down the line. His concept of Total Quality Control extends the administrative function to include the measurement and control of quality at every stage, from customer specification and sales, through design, engineering, assembly and shipment. In *Total Quality Control*, published in 1983, he states that 'Quality is in its essence a way of managing the organisation'. Today, Feigenbaum sees quality as having become the single, most important force leading to organisational success and company growth in national and international markets.

Feigenbaum teaches that effective management of the factors affecting quality means that control procedures must be in place throughout the production (or service) process;

- New design control;
- Incoming material control;
- Product control;
- Special process studies.

In *Quality Control: Principles, Practices and Administration*, he defines quality control as

> An effective system for co-ordinating the quality maintenance and quality improvement efforts of the various groups in an organisation so as to enable production at the most economical levels which allow for full customer satisfaction.

He stresses that quality does not mean 'best' but 'best for the customer use and selling price'.

Control is seen as a management tool with four steps:

- Setting quality standards;
- Appraising conformance to these standards;
- Acting when the standards are exceeded;
- Planning for improvement in the standards.

Feigenbaum argues that statistical techniques should be employed whenever and wherever they may be useful, but that they are only part of the overall administrative quality control system and not the system itself. The details of the quality programme will be specific for each organisation but certain basic areas of attention will be common to all. Total Quality Control is seen as providing the structure and tools for managing quality so that there is a continuous emphasis throughout the organisation on quality leadership.

The need for quality-mindedness throughout all levels is emphasised and the quality control organisation is seen as both:

- a channel for communication for product quality information;
- a means of participation in the overall plant quality programme.

A Total Quality System is defined by him as:

> The agreed company-wide and plant-wide operating work structure, documented in effective, integrated technical and managerial procedures, for guiding the co-ordinated actions of the people, the machines, and the information of the company and plan in the best and most practical ways to assure customer quality satisfaction and economical costs of quality.

Operating quality costs can be divided into:

- Prevention costs – including quality planning;
- Appraisal costs – including inspection;

- Internal failure costs – including scrap and rework;
- External failure costs – including warranty costs, product recall.

Reductions in operating quality costs result from establishing a total quality system for two reasons:

- Lack of existing effective customer-oriented standards may mean that current product quality is not optimal, given use;
- Expenditure on prevention can lead to a severalfold reduction in internal and external failure costs.

Dr Feigenbaum was founding chairperson of the International Academy for Quality and is a past president of the American Society for Quality Control, which presented him with the Edwards Medal and the Lancaster Award for his international contributions to quality and productivity. In 1988, he was appointed to the board which oversees the Malcolm Baldrige National Quality Award Programme and, in 1991, the fortieth anniversary edition of *Total Quality Control* was published.

Dr Kaoru Ishikawa

Dr Ishikawa was born in 1915 and graduated from Tokyo University in 1939 with a degree in applied chemistry. His name will perhaps be best known to many people from the Ishikawa Diagram, otherwise known as the Cause and Effect Diagram or the Fishbone Diagram. Ishikawa invented the diagram (in 1952) to supplement the other tools and techniques that he advocated for the measurement, control and improvement of processes in (mainly) Japanese companies until his death in 1989.

After the war, he returned to Tokyo University and in 1948 began to study statistical methods. By 1949, he had joined JUSE's Quality Control Research Group and, following Deming's visit in 1950, began teaching the application of statistical methods for quality control, making it compulsory for his engineering students at the university.

Ishikawa's contribution to the turnround of Japan's industry since the war cannot, perhaps, be overstated. As well as teaching the techniques of quality control directly to all levels within diverse organisations, he pioneered the Quality Circle movement in Japan, initiated quality conferences, contributed regularly to quality journals and worked closely with the Japanese Industrial Standards Committee which led to him becoming chairperson of the Japanese Chapter of the International Standards Organisation in 1977.

Ishikawa had the rare ability to adopt technical methods, and make them accessible and palatable to all levels within an organisation. In particular, he championed the use of what are commonly called the Seven Tools of Quality Control.

- Pareto charts – to prioritise action;
- Cause and Effect diagrams – to identify causes of variation;
- Stratification – to divide data into subsets;
- Check sheets – for data collection;
- Histograms – to display variation graphically;
- Scatter diagrams – to confirm relationships between two factors;
- Shewhart's control charts and graphs – to monitor and control variation.

The same set of tools were used on a team basis at all levels and by all functions within organisations for the measurement, evaluation, control and improvement of all business activities, not just for quality control of the product. Furthermore, because the output from the use of the tools is graphical, the information displayed can be understood by all, helping to reduce misunderstandings and obviate communication problems.

Ishikawa's book, *Guide to Quality Control*, Tokyo, Asian Productivity Organisation, 1976, based on articles written for the *Quality Control for the Foreman* journal, is a classic text describing the use of these tools. One of Ishikawa's pet themes, highlighted in the book, is the accurate collection and use of data; he argued that all data should be treated with suspicion and historical databases should be ignored. Data should be collected as and where they are needed.

Company-wide quality

Ishikawa was a key player in the Company-wide Quality Control movement which started in Japan around 1955, following the visits of Deming and Juran. Company-wide quality control necessitates measurement by all. Everyone studies statistical methods. Every function and all levels participate in the improvement process; research, design, engineering, manufacturing, sales, clerical, personnel, etc. Quality Control concepts and methods are used to measure, monitor and improve incoming raw materials, manufacturing processes, personnel issues and sales problems. In Ishikawa's concept, quality does not only mean the quality of the product, but also after-sales service, quality of management, the company itself and the human being.

As a result, the following occurs.

- Product quality improves and becomes uniform. Defects are reduced.
- Product reliability is improved.
- Cost is reduced.
- Productivity increases and it becomes possible to make rational production schedules.
- Wasteful work and rework are reduced.
- Technique is established and improved.
- Expenses for inspection and testing are reduced.
- Contracts between vendor and vendee are rationalised.
- The sales market is enlarged.
- Better relationships are established between departments.

- False data and reports are reduced.
- Discussions are carried out more freely and democratically.
- Meetings are operated more smoothly.
- Repairs and installations of equipment and facilities are done more rationally.
- Human relations are improved.

Quality Control Circles

Quality Control (QC) circles are a major feature of company-wide quality control and illustrate Ishikawa's commitment to education and measurement for all. In 1962 Ishikawa became chairperson of the editorial board of a low-price journal entitled *Quality Control for the Foreman*. This was published by JUSE and built on the success of another regular JUSE publication, *Statistical Quality Control*, which originated in 1950. The purpose of the new magazine was to get the message and techniques of quality measurement to the operators in the front line. QC circles began in Japan as study groups – workers and their foremen being encouraged to read and discuss the concepts and methods advocated in *Quality Control for the Foreman*, and then to try the approaches in their own work areas.

The nature and role of circles varies between companies, but the following is a general guide. They typically consist of small groups of five to ten people from the same work area who meet voluntarily on a regular basis to discuss, investigate, measure and analyse work-related problems. The circle is led by a foreman or one of the workers and the seven tools of quality control are used. Depending on the organisation, solutions to problems identified by the circle are either presented to management for authorisation before implementation, or the team has authority to implement directly. Circle members receive no direct financial reward for their improvements.

The aims of the QC circle activities are to:

- Contribute to the improvement and development of the enterprise;

- Respect human relations and build a happy workshop offering job satisfaction;
- Deploy human capabilities fully and draw out infinite potential.

The QC circle concept spread rapidly, both within manufacturing companies and also into service organisations. Encouraged by books, seminars, lectures, annual conferences and visits to other organisations, the number of individuals involved in circles activity in Japan is now in excess of ten million. Ishikawa was central to masterminding much of this growth and in laying down the ground rules for circle activities.

Ishikawa is often regarded as the 'father of Japanese quality'. He was awarded the Deming Prize, the Nihon Keizai Press Prize, the Industrial Standardisation Prize and the Grant Award. The latter was presented by the American Society for Quality Control in 1971 in recognition for his education programme on quality control.

Dr Genichi Taguchi and Dr Shigeo Shingo

Taguchi and Shingo are two further Japanese quality gurus whose ideas contributed tremendously to Japan's post-war turnround. Both evolved methods for the prevention of quality problems in manufacture and for the design of efficient processes – but used very different approaches. Their methods are now finding increasing use in the West.

Taguchi

Genichi Taguchi was born in Japan in 1924. When the Nippon Telephone and Telegraph Company established its Electrical Communications Laboratory (ECL) in 1949, he was recruited to improve the efficiency of their research and development activities. His first book was published in 1951 and earned him the Deming award for literature on quality. The book introduced statistical methods for minimising the number of trials or tests that need to be carried out in order to arrive at a satisfactory design. In 1954–5, Taguchi visited the Indian Statistical Institute where he conducted several experiments, and also met Shewhart and Fisher. Part of Taguchi's methodology is based on the work begun by Fisher in England in the 1920s, but expanded and adapted for industrial applications.

During the 12 years that Taguchi spent with ECL, he consulted widely among many Japanese companies, including Toyota. Likewise Ishikawa, he has been able to simplify complex statistical methods and make them comprehensible to non-academics. Taguchi's methods, which in essence build quality into processes and products at the design stage, were therefore available to many Japanese companies from the 1950s. The diagram shown in Figure 3.2 illustrates the relative contributions of the different approaches to quality control used in Japan since the Second World War.

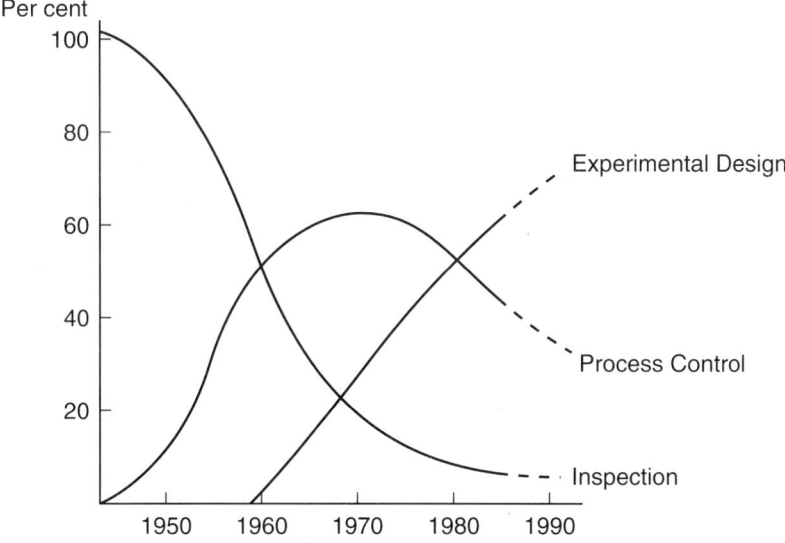

Figure 3.2

Taguchi methods can be used for trouble-shooting in production, but their main application is in the design of new production processes and, increasingly, new products. Within a process, the number of factors that contribute to the quality and consistency of the output can be many. Which are the important ones and how important are they? Are they always important or only under certain conditions? To test out and measure the effect of all of the possible combinations of variables and at different levels would be an impossible task. How long can you wait to get a new product to market?

Conventionally, the need to get new products to market quickly can mean that processes are set up based on previous experience, a few trials that nearly worked and with 'fingers crossed' as production starts, in the hope of meeting the agreed deadline. As problems occur, they are dealt with as far as possible by problem solving and at great cost in terms of defectives produced, time wasted, customer dissatisfaction etc. The process variables are subsequently 'twiddled' in an effort to improve consistency of output and minimise the production of defectives.

Instead, Taguchi's approach uses a standard set of tables to optimise the number of experimental trails that need to be carried out initially. These 'orthogonal arrays' reduce the number of tests dramatically by giving an experimental design pattern which does not measure the effect of every possible combination or level of factors, but gives sufficient measure on each for decisions to be made. Further trials to home in more precisely on the optimum levels can be made if required. As an example of the power of the method: 7 different factors each at 2 levels would require 128 experiments if tackled conventionally; Taguchi uses just 8. For 6 factors at 5 levels, equivalent to 15,625 combinations, Taguchi would carry out 25 experiments initially.

By carrying out the design experiments, the optimum level and relative importance of each variable is established with regard to the sensitivity of the process to environmental and other uncontrollable factors. Efficient and robust processes can then be set up using these data, and Statistical Process Control can be used to monitor and control quality characteristics in the critical areas identified.

The 'Quality Loss Function', developed by Taguchi in the early 1970s, may be used to measure and evaluate design decisions on a financial basis. The cost element is defined as 'loss imparted by the product to society from the time the product is shipped'. The loss includes not only the normal company costs of scrap, rework, downtime, warranty etc., but also costs to the customer in terms of poor product performance and reliability, which themselves may result in the manu-facturer losing future business. To minimise this loss to society, the variation from the target, for any particular quality charac-teristic, must also be minimised – usually at extra cost. By using the quality loss function – a mathematical formula – decisions can be made to determine whether additional costs in produc-tion will actually prove to be worthwhile in the market place. For this reason, the loss function is usually used at the last phase of designing a new product or process, after the design has already been optimised as fully as possible.

Since 1980, more and more American companies have imple-mented Taguchi methodology – including Xerox, Ford and ITT. In Europe, with one or two exceptions – such as Lucas – Taguchi's approach found little application until, in 1987, the Institute of Statisticians organised a conference in London to publicise the methods. The UK Taguchi Club (now part of the Quality Methods Association) was formed later that year.

Shingo

Born in Japan in 1909, Shigeo Shingo is perhaps not as well known in the West as Ishikawa and Taguchi, although the impact of his work, especially in Japan, has been immense. After graduating in Mechanical Engineering at Yamanashi

Technical College in 1930, he joined the Taipei Railway Factory in Taiwan where he introduced the methods of scientific management. In 1945 he became a professional consultant with the Japan Management Association where, as Education Department chairperson in 1951, he first became aware of statistical quality control techniques.

From 1955 he was responsible for industrial engineering and factory improvement training at Toyota Motor Company. In the period between 1956 and 1958, while working at Mitsubishi Heavy Industries in Nagasaki, Shingo was responsible for halving the time for hull assembly of a 65,000 ton supertanker from four months to two months. His methods quickly spread to other Japanese shipyards. In 1959 he left the Japan Management Association and established the Institute of Management Improvement.

From 1961 Shingo started to develop poka-yoke systems. Poka-yoke literally means mistake-proofing and was the name he adopted for the technique after he received complaints for calling the method fool-proofing (baka-yoke). Many engineers and managers will be aware of the basic idea. In the West, we often see this approach where safety is an issue, but in Japan it is also used extensively where quality is the main concern. Interestingly, poka-yoke systems, by using devices which prevent defects from occurring, obviate the need for measurement. Poka-yoke systems in general involve two phases: the detection aspect and the regulatory aspect. Detection can be accomplished by various means: physical contact, limit switches, photoelectric cells, press-sensitive switches, thermostats etc. Regulation can be by either giving a warning (e.g. flashing light, alarm buzzer) or by taking control (prevention, automatically shutting a machine down) – or both.

Shingo distinguished between 'errors' and 'defects', the latter being caused by the former. He recognised that people do make mistakes, for a variety of reasons, but that errors need not result in defects. His method is to stop the process whenever an error occurs and to establish the source of the error by inspection, and then to prevent its recurrence. Poka-yoke devices, in effect give 100 per cent inspection, but during the process when prevention is possible and not after the event when it is too late. Using Shingo's concept of Zero Quality Control, zero defects can be achieved.

Shingo had been a firm believer in the application of statistical process control since he first learned about it. Gradually, as he did more and more work with poka-yoke systems, his enthusiasm for Statistical Process Control waned. Improvement from statistical methods comes from the detection and measurement of defects and a reaction to them; his methods prevent defects. Furthermore, statistical methods use sampling techniques; his poka-yoke methods allow for 100 per cent inspection and make measurement unnecessary.

By 1977, he was finally released from the spell of statistical methods when a plant in Matsushita's Washing Machine Division had 7 months of defect-free operation in their drain-pipe assembly line involving 23 workers producing 30,000 units per month. Since then, many more companies have run for months without producing defects by using Singo's Zero Quality Control methods.

Poka-yoke systems improve process efficiency, save waste and reduce costs; critical factors for measurement and improvement in any organisation. In 1969 while working for Toyota, Shingo developed a system known as Single-Minute Exchange of Die or SMED. This improvement methodology similarly reduces waste. The purpose of SMED is to minimise the amount of time taken when making changeovers. It reduces downtime and increases production flexibility, obviating the need for long production runs and large batches. Inventory can be reduced dramatically, as there is less need to maintain stock to cover for the hold-ups.

At Toyota, the set-up time for a 1,000 ton press was four hours, twice as long as it took Volkswagen in West Germany.

Within six months, Shingo had reduced Toyota's set-up time for the operation to one-and-a-half-hours. Following this initial success, a new target was given – three minutes! Shingo achieved this within a further three months! Other examples show set-up times being reduced from six hours to six minutes and work-in-progress inventory being slashed by 90 per cent.

Set-up time is made up of two elements which can be measured separately: internal set-up time, when the machine must be stopped, and external set-up time, when the machine need not be stopped. The optimisation process involves converting as much internal set-up time to external set-up time – and then relentlessly improving both aspects. The improvements are made by a variety of simplification and de-skilling methods: jigs, clamps, quick-release fastenings, standardisation of fittings, etc.

When production hold-ups are reduced dramatically by the application of SMED techniques and when output can be virtually guaranteed by zero defect production, just-in-time (JIT) operating methods, Kanban and non-stock production become possible. Shingo was a key player in the introduction of these approaches within several companies and Toyota's production system in particular.

Shingo was awarded the Yellow Ribbon Decoration in 1970 for his services in improving production. He wrote more than 14 major books, several of which have now been translated into English and other European languages. Shigeo Shingo died in 1990.

THE EARLY APPROACH BY THE JAPANESE TO BENCHMARKING

The first recorded references to the actual physical process of Benchmarking itself can be traced to the early 1950s when the Japanese paid many visits to Western organisations. Paying particular attention to the manufacturing processes of those organisations situated in the US and in Western Europe the Japanese excelled in the absorption of best business practices into their own manufacturing industries. An operation which has effectively resulted in the International reputation of the Japanese in the commercial market.

The Japanese supplemented their visits to Western organisations with the importation of both Western technology and business practices. This was achieved by the contractual importation of Western knowledge, and between the periods of 1952 through to March 1984, no fewer than 42,000 contracts were entered into by the Japanese. These contracts represented the best technology and 'know-how' that the West possessed and the Japanese then put this information to their own advantage, once again using the process of adoption and adaptation. This pattern of extensively purchasing critical technology lasted until the late 1960s, by which time the Japanese were catching up with Western organisations.

The success of the Japanese in using Western technology to Benchmark their own performance against, is evident by their international reputation in the commercial arena. It is rather difficult to envisage how the Japanese, a country devastated by the Second World War, could possibly have reached this stage without both the contractual importation of knowledge or by visits to the West in search of best practices. A tremendous amount of foresight then has been shown by the Japanese in utilising these two sources of knowledge to their own advantage. Clearly lessons are to be learnt in the West by building upon these practices used by the Japanese to improve their own performance and share of the commercial market.

BENCHMARKING – THE NATURAL PROGRESSION

Throughout recorded history people have been improving the

quality of their products and processes, and organisational and human performance. Today, Total Quality Management is a means of improving service both to internal and external customers. There is, within Total Quality Management, a continuous commitment to the self-improving organisation. The principles of Total Quality Management with regard to culture, organisational strategy and a documented quality management system all constitute the self-improving organisation. They all require commitment to training, education and general indoctrination into the quality initiative. The self-improving organisation is therefore one in which the rest position is essentially one of improvement.

Like other tools used in a Quality programme, Benchmarking has an extremely important role to play. Its primary purpose is the establishment and identification of areas of importance which may then be used as a channel for driving continuous improvement by closing the 'Benchmarking gap'. For many businesses today competition is on the world stage and in the crucial areas selected the only sensible goals are those which constitute world best practices. Benchmarking is a method for making sure that the targets aimed for are relevant to market demands and not arbitrarily established by 'a finger in the air' or extrapolation from last year's achievements.

Total Quality Management, as developed from the ideas of the Quality Gurus, undoubtedly does improve both the internal and external performance of an organisation by setting targets and goals to be achieved. However, we must move on from this and look at global practice in order to keep up with competitors. The most useful method of doing this is with the use of external comparisons. The only way to drive an organisation to excellence is to ensure that they keep their eye upon their competitors and world's best practice.

4 THE BIRTH OF BENCHMARKING – THE XEROX APPROACH

INTRODUCTION

As we saw in Chapter 1, the Xerox Corporation of America adopted a vigorous approach to Benchmarking in 1979, when they found that their competitors were able to sell products more cheaply than Xerox could make them. The approach they adopted has now become the model for others to follow.

In Robert C. Camp's 1989 book, *Benchmarking: The Search for Industry Best Practices that Lead to Superior Performance* Milwaukee, ASQC Quality Press, 1989, he cites the definition put forward by David T. Kearns, CEO of the Xerox Corporation as:

> . . . the continuous process of measuring products, services and practices against the toughest competitors or those companies recognized as industry leaders.

Benchmarking is a key element in Xerox's business strategy. At the highest level in the business, 10 critical parameters have been defined; at the next level, a further 13 have been identified; each of these 23 critical success factors has a Benchmark performance against it – what Xerox consider to be the best of the best – and these are continuously updated.

Every aspect of Xerox's business is Benchmarked and some of their reported successes in diverse areas are:

- Incoming parts acceptance improved to 99.5 per cent;
- Inventory reduced by two-thirds;
- Engineering drawings per person doubled;
- Marketing productivity improved by one-third;
- Service labour cost reduced by 30 per cent;
- Distribution productivity increased by 8–10 per cent.

An early major Benchmarking exercise involved L.L. Bean, the American mail order company and retailer of outdoor clothing. For their warehousing/distribution operation, Xerox identified L.L. Bean as the functional leader to Benchmark against, because of its superiority in the areas of order-picking and warehousing. Even though the business area is completely different, the basic operation carried out by the function is very similar.

THE BENCHMARKING PROCESS

Xerox have a clearly-defined ten-step process for Benchmarking:

1 Identify Benchmarking subject;
2 Identify comparative companies;
3 Determine data collection method and collect data;
4 Determine current competitive gap;
5 Project future performance;
6 Communicate findings and gain acceptance;
7 Establish functional goals;
8 Develop action plans;
9 Implement plans and monitor progress;
       ‥‥te Benchmark.

                    ice, the area where most people go wrong is at
                    within Xerox, there are still people who make
                    l consider that they are carrying out a

Benchmarking exercise. However, unless the good ideas observed during a visit are in line with the improvement priorities established back at base, there will be little chance of them being implemented. Without a clear definition of what it is that needs changing, without prioritised goals for improvement, any visits are unfocused.

Improvement opportunities are identified by recognising the critical processes which deliver the critical success factors in the market place. The critical processes are then analysed and the improvement opportunities identified are prioritised. For example, Xerox have four business objectives as a corporation:

- Customer satisfaction;
- Employee satisfaction;
- Return on assets;
- Market share.

For return on assets, a Cause and Effect diagram has been used to analyse and give greater understanding of the contributory factors, and how attention should be prioritised for benchmarking activity. Within their Marketing Group, ten areas were identified:

- Customer Marketing;
- Customer Engagement;
- Order Fulfilment;
- Product Maintenance;
- Billing and Collection;
- Financial Management;
- Asset Management;
- Business Management;
- Information Technology;
- Human Resource Management.

Within these 10 areas, 67 sub-processes were identified. Each of the sub-processes became candidates for the improvement process.

SELECTING COMPANIES TO BENCHMARK AGAINST

To get information on suitable Benchmarking companies, Xerox subscribe to ABI Information, an American management database. They also have access to a large technical database. When searching for someone to Benchmark against for their warehousing/distribution operation in 1981, they collected and analysed material from 11 organisations. Databases were consulted, magazines and trade journals covering a three-year period were reviewed, professional associations were asked and consulting firms were contacted.

Although Benchmarking is carried out internally and against direct competitors, it is by carrying out functional and generic Benchmarking that Xerox have identified their greatest improvement opportunities. Xerox used American Express as their Benchmark for invoicing processes, Florida Power and Light for their quality management processes, and Ford and Cummins Engines for their factory layout.

For supplier development, Honda Manufacturing of America has been Benchmarked. At the time of the study, Xerox had ten engineers working with suppliers to improve quality. Honda, meanwhile, a comparative company in terms . of costs, have a dedicated supplier development team of 96, over half of whom are graduate engineers! And this for a key supplier base of 216 for assembled parts, which is somewhat less than Xerox's list of suppliers.

According to Roger Sugden of Rank Xerox Ltd., the following points are key for successful Benchmarking.

- It is essential to understand your own processes thoroughly.
- Visits are not arranged until sufficient desk research has been carried out to ensure that the companies selected are the best that can be found.
- The focus must be on Industry Best Practices.

- There must be a willingness to share information. Reciprocal visits are arranged if required.
- Sensitive information is always kept confidential.
- Getting the process owners or operators to carry out the Benchmarking studies is seen as being critical; trying to involve people after the study is too late.
- Do not concentrate on outcomes; it is the practices and processes that need to be understood.
- Benchmarking must be a continuous process; the competition is constantly changing.
- There must be a willingness to change based on the Benchmark findings.

BENCHMARKING AND TOTAL QUALITY MANAGEMENT (TQM)

These observations are supplemented by Chas McCann, Director of Business Quality and Technical Support at Rank Xerox, who emphasises that the incorporation of Benchmarking within TQM is not easy. Some of the problems may be anticipated and thus the impact can be minimised. Accordingly, good practice at Xerox is as follows:

1 Tie projects to the corporate goals or priorities. A demonstration of linkage should be inspected and evidence of activities within the planning process should be provided. Do not stray outside the corporate goals and planning process – Benchmarking hotels in the Bahamas may provide some interesting facts, as well as fun, but may not be strictly appropriate.

2 Differentiate between competitive analysis and Benchmarking. Good applications of a Benchmarking

process will determine gaps in performance – competitive analysis will give more superficial information.

3 Detailed preparation work is required to avoid waste of effort and there are two aspects in particular to consider here.

(a) Benchmarking within the design cycle may be carried out too late and result in a cost reduction instead of cost prevention by the introduction of cost-effective designs.

(b) During the planning process and the gathering of Benchmarking information there will be a risk of committing manpower and cost in pursuit of wrong targets, metrics or processes. One should use visit checklists etc. to ensure focus on the right areas.

4 Continuous improvement can be achieved if inspection and encouragement is provided to improve processes, methods and practices. Without this inspection, the roll out and incorporation of Benchmarking may falter.

As the first winners of the European Quality Award, Bernard Fournier, Managing Director of Rank Xerox (UK), pointed to Benchmarking as a key element in their success. Specifically, in his presentation on receiving the Award from King Juan Carlos of Spain in Madrid on 15 October 1992, he described Xerox's use of Internal Benchmarking as a key element. By 'Benchmarking with themselves', sharing best practices with the 22 other Rank Xerox companies in Europe, the company has learned how to combat the 'not invented here syndrome'. Director of Quality and Customer Satisfaction, Rafael Florez, also described the use of surveys, including an anonymous one asking customers who their top supplier is in a specific target market. Finally, Bernard Fournier concluded by making particular reference to the company's unified Health and Safety Standard and achievements in exceeding the Du pont industry Benchmark of 0.5 incidents per 200 khrs.

The value of this approach should not be doubted. The

company has progressed from being rated as top vendor in 9 out of 75 business sectors in 1989 to being first in 62 sectors in 1992, while customer satisfaction has increased from 71 to 97 per cent in the same period.

5 WHAT IT'S ALL ABOUT –
THE BENCHMARKING PROCESS

INTRODUCTION

In previous chapters we have examined the nature of the Benchmarking Boom and something of the role of Benchmarking in the modern world. We have looked at the Total Quality Management (TQM) revolution in management thinking with its focus on internal business processes, and considered the important and revolutionary approach of focusing on such processes in order to identify the potential for improvement. We also considered Quality Measurement, the need for a unified concept of measurement deployed throughout the organisation, the need to measure processes rather than just inputs or outputs and the need for external comparisons. We have also looked at the pre-history of Benchmarking, looking at the various Quality Gurus and the history of Quality Measurement. Finally, we have culminated so far in the Xerox story, a case of Benchmarking for Survival that shaped the Benchmarking Boom of today.

To summarise, then, the keys to Benchmarking, Western management's move towards TQM has itself represented a natural evolution from naïve ideas of product conformity to specification, often achieved by inspection, through concepts of Quality Assurance achieved by documentation and control of the processes involved in the production, delivery and management of product or service, to the concept of the self-improving organisation. TQM is seen as primarily a management-led approach in which top management commitment is essential.

The emphasis is on Quality in all aspects and functions of the organisation's operation, not just in the provision of a major service or product to the external end customer. Employee awareness and motivation are essential. Employees are responsible for ensuring Quality in terms of satisfying the customer in all they do, and the approach is one of prevention of errors and faults rather than detection and correction. Typically, cultural change in the organisation from reactive to proactive, and from an inspection to a prevention approach and to one of involvement, is necessary. Organisational change is also typically needed. A strong emphasis is also placed on identifying internal customers and meeting their needs. Emphasis must be placed on supplier/customer relationships. In such programmes, teamwork is often used to ensure involvement and a movement to a continuous improvement culture.

The second key to Benchmarking is the importance of business processes, as identified within most TQM approaches, rather than emphasising the classical functional divisions of the organisation such as Finance, Stores, Sales etc. The organisation is seen as a set of major and minor business processes, each major process being concerned with delivery of a service or product to an end customer and, typically, running across all or many of the functional areas of the organisation. Such a process analysis, makes us realise that typically the processes of the business have no single owners and that the end customer has to rely on satisfactory completion of process steps and communication by all the functional areas involved. By concentrating on the processes instead, we are able to identify process inefficiencies such as delays or queuing at process 'bottle-necks', lack of control or checking of a crucial process step, situations where the process is itself unable to cope or there is no clear process procedure and places where responsibility for process activities is not clear. We can identify measurement points in the process, verify how well we are currently doing and plan the introduction of improvements using the measurement points to monitor the improvements being achieved. Concentrating on the process enables us to monitor the internal workings of the system and not just concentrate on the end product that the customer sees which is often too late.

The third key to Benchmarking is the limitation of the TQM model as it has evolved in the West. The crude model concentrates clearly on the need to improve, the importance of the customer, cultural change, of the continuous nature of improvement, on teamwork and on the participation of everyone. While the programme should be steered by top management and the way forward planned, monitored, reviewed and readjusted, the basic data input in this measurement process is often taken naïvely as performance against improvement targets and past performance. While this is a good approach to get started, to break through the cultural barriers created by the mentality of conformance to requirement rather than self-improvement, it itself begs the question as to whether management really has a wide enough view to focus on the improvement process and the real issues. After all, if management accepts the fact that a TQM programme is necessary, it is, in a sense, admitting that its management skills in the past have not been perfect. It is admitting that there is a need to get everyone aligned in the organisation to improve, to rethink the organisation and the way it does business, to hear the voice of the people that really do the job and the voice of the customers. A caveat of this admission is that management's and the workforce's own conception of what needs to be improved and by how much, might not be as appropriate as it would like to think. Management can set the priorities against strategic objectives, but it really needs to convince itself that it is not missing anything, that its competitors are not stealing a march on it, that there is not a missing ingredient in the way that we do things compared to the way that our competitors do them that really gives them the advantage. And this comparison, of course, is not just limited to our competitors, but to world best practice; on any-thing we can transfer from another area of activity into that of our own.

The fourth key to Benchmarking is that once we have accepted this need to study our competitors and world best practice, and, also, the importance of internal business pro-cesses, then we must bring these two themes together and systematically examine all our internal processes and perform-ance in comparison to external Benchmarks. This taxonomy of our internal operations is a necessary requirement for a coherent improvement process.

Finally, the fifth and last key to Benchmarking is the Xerox story – Benchmarking for survival. The experience and exper-tise Xerox created has contributed enormously to the concept of Benchmarking as we know it today. However, it is not, of course, necessary to wait until the last possible moment in the fight for survival to start the process.

THE NEED FOR CHANGE

Before we go through the steps in the Benchmarking process it is necessary to make some general observations. There can be many problems and pitfalls in Benchmarking. Not least are the usual ones encountered when organisations decide to 'imple-ment' the other aspects of TQM.

Commitment from the top is absolutely essential if the approach is to be successful and if improvements are to follow from the comparative measuring exercise. Times vary greatly but, generally, the initial research activity may take between 6 and 18 months to complete, and the level of resource that needs to be committed can be very high. Then the hard part – making the improvements – begins. Benchmarking is no quick fix with instant payback; unless senior management show patience and take leadership for the change process, the whole activity is likely to become another 'flavour of the month' – resulting in frustration and apathy.

There must be a belief in the need to change. This belief is likely to be reinforced when comparisons with market leaders are made, but it is management's responsibility to generate enthusiasm for improvements and to overcome resistance to change throughout the organisation. Benchmarking is a tool to help the change process and not the preserve of a few élite specialists. The people who will be asked to make changes following the Benchmarking exercise must be involved with the process from the beginning. Their input will help to prevent silly mistakes being made during the study and they will recognise the need for improvement when the comparisons are made.

If their first introduction to the Benchmarking exercise comes from the analysis and consists of 'Company X can produce twice as much as you can in half the time', without any reference to how, then the reaction is likely to be somewhat different. Not everyone can be part of the investigation team, but it is important to keep people informed of the progress being made by communicating as much information as possible to those who will be involved at the implementation stage.

Benchmarking is a tool for people who are serious about making improvements. Training is necessary, both at the awareness level and for practical application. The Benchmarking process needs to be planned, steered, monitored and reviewed if maximum benefits are to accrue and the exercise is not to deteriorate into a 'nice to know' outcome. Trying to do too much too quickly will result in information overload and confused priorities; to allow people to become familiar with the methodology, two or three key areas for investigation are quite sufficient initially. Senior management support and recognition will then act as a spur for further activity.

WHAT IS TO BE BENCHMARKED?

Benchmarking is not about making visits to other companies to 'try to pick up one or two ideas that may be useful somewhere'. Instead, it is centred around planned research which has been focused by a company's recognition that it needs to make improvements in critical business areas.

Improvement, generally, is initiated by asking the following questions.

- Where do we want to be?
- Where are we now?
- What do we need to do to get from here to there?

Any activity that can be measured can be Benchmarked, but most companies will start with those areas where they know they need to be competitive to remain in business. The company should have a clear mission statement or list of business goals which is used to focus improvement activity. Customer satisfaction is high on most company priority lists, as is the need for a low-cost operation. Deciding these broad areas partly answers the question 'Where do we want to be?' These broad areas, however, need to be broken down into more specific activities that can be measured. What are the processes that deliver customer satisfaction? What processes eat up the costs? The more precisely you define what you need to measure, the more useful will be the information that you gather to compare it with.

What things are important to customers? What will help them to be successful? How good is the service currently given? What factors cause customer dissatisfaction? An analysis of customer complaints and warranty claims can give some guidance here and, of course, the customer can be asked directly. Questionnaires can be sent out and review workshops can be organised. 'Reliability' is a major requirement of most customers, but what does it mean and how is it measured? The answer may be by on-time delivery, performance or by levels of defect-free product. What key measures are already in place to monitor both current performance and the hoped-for improvement? What is your current performance in these areas and what is your current practice for achieving those performances?

The Cost of Quality approach for identifying areas for improvement is not dealt with in detail in this book, but common areas for Benchmarking are the related areas of stock levels, work in progress, waste and reject levels. Again, the cost (measures) for each of these areas must be known, but also it is essential to understand the processes and practices that lead to these costs being incurred. A thorough analysis of what actually happens is necessary, not a blind acceptance of a theoretical process model.

At the end of the day, you will need to understand how and why organisations that you have Benchmarked have achieved their superiority, not just the levels of attainment that they have achieved. Comparing numbers will not help you to compete; it is necessary to compare the practices that have given rise to the numbers.

Emphasis has been placed on this initial step because, in the experience of leading Benchmarking organisations like Xerox, it is here where most companies get it wrong. Until organisations understand their processes fully and how those processes deliver the current performance in key areas, it is meaningless to make comparisons with other organisations.

When the process is understood, and the criticial activities are known and measured, the 'Where are we now?' question has been answered. It should be clear where improvements could be made by investigating best practice elsewhere, i.e. the area to be Benchmarked. It is essential to make sure, though, that the subjects chosen for Benchmarking are based on current market demands and not just on areas that the company considers to be important. In the production of electronic components, for example, a defect-free supply is perhaps now almost taken for granted; the requirements may be instead primarily for service differentiation and time to market.

WHO TO BENCHMARK AGAINST?

Deciding on who to Benchmark against depends on the subject chosen for Benchmarking, the resources that can be made available and the challenge that an organisation is prepared to undertake. In general, there are often seen to be four different types of Benchmarking; each approach has its own advantages and disadvantages.

- **Internal Benchmarking** involves making comparisons with other parts of the same organisation. It can be with other departments, other sites, other companies within the same group, either in the same country or abroad. This type of Benchmarking is usually straightforward to arrange and fairly common. It is relatively easy to obtain all of the information necessary for a good comparison to be made. If the operations are similar across the different sites, the data will be instantly relevant and usable, but it is unlikely to yield improvements which meet world best practice.

- **Competitor Benchmarking** is much more difficult. Any information obtained is likely to be very relevant but, for reasons of confidentiality, it will be almost impossible to get a full picture of how a direct competitor operates. Looking at outputs and available figures can give some information, but they can also mislead if the processes that deliver the outputs cannot be determined. Some of the larger organisations, however, do exchange information in selected areas in the interest of jointly coming to terms with best practice.

- **Functional Benchmarking** involves making comparisons with typically non-competitive organisations which carry out the same functional activity that you are interested in. Examples are warehousing, procurement, catering etc. This type of Benchmarking has several advantages: functional leaders are easy to identify in many areas; confidentiality is not usually an issue; approaches which may be novel for your industry can be discovered; two-way partnerships can be developed. Weighing against these are likely to be problems in adopting and adapting their practices for your operation.

- **Generic Benchmarking** goes a step further and may compare business processes which cut across various functions and in quite different industries. Opportunities discovered by this process are likely to be the most innovative and to create breakthroughs for unprecedented improvement. However, the integration of novel concepts into a different industry is also likely to be the most challenging.

The type of Benchmarking and organisations chosen to Benchmark against depends on many factors. If your organisation is large and generally looked on as being a market leader, then the requirement is obviously different from that demanded by a smaller company with perhaps less experience of making quality improvements. The former will have a real need to search out best practices, whereas the latter will probably find it easy to identify improvement opportunties by observing the practices of almost any successful company.

Similarly, the level of resource that can be, and needs to be, committed in each case will be different. It makes sense to limit initial visits to local companies if possible; not only will the time and cost be less, but also problems associated with language and cultural differences will be avoided. Obviously, where the opportunity presents itself, internal Benchmarking is the ideal place to start. Kodak do this between their sites, as do Philips. The whole process is relatively easy to manage and gives experience in the technique.

For other types of Benchmarking, there are various sources

of information which can aid in the identification of organisations to compare against. A simple starting point is the knowledge already within your own company; the marketing function, for example. Then, customers, suppliers and other contacts within the same industry can usually contribute good ideas. Consultants, academics and other industry observers can be asked who they think are the leaders in any particular area. Trade journals, magazines, books and other library material are useful, and ideas can also be picked up at conferences, workshops and seminars.

One point should be mentioned. How do you know that the company which you have selected for Benchmarking really represents best practice? The answer is that you don't – and perhaps never will. If the research you have carried out indicates that it is the best you have yet come across, and their performance is better than yours, then proceed to the next step. Perhaps somewhere there is someone a little better; you may discover them at a later date. It is important to halt the research, temporarily at least, and to start making improvements.

Some companies have sidestepped the issue of who to Benchmark against by opting to use as a Benchmark the idealised requirements of the Malcolm Baldrige Quality Award. In Japan, companies have prepared themselves for the Deming Award in a similar way, even though the requirements are less clearly defined and structured. The new European Quality Award goes beyond Malcolm Baldrige in some areas and obviously it, too, presents an opportunity for making comparisons.

COLLECTING THE BENCHMARKING DATA

Although the most valuable information will be obtained by the direct exchange of data with other companies, much useful material can be gleaned from indirect sources. The sources mentioned in the previous section can be utilised, supplemented by information from annual reports, public databases, research institutes, government agencies etc. However, one must beware, since some of the data obtained by these means will be out of date or may be erroneous for other reasons.

Before descending upon other organisations, it is vital to carry out as much desk research as possible in order to optimise the value of any visits. To supplement other sources, questionnaires can be prepared and sent to potential Benchmark companies, for completion and return before the visit. Also, internal discussions should be held before the visits to establish the extent of current knowledge and to focus the requirements of the investigation so that a comprehensive checklist can be prepared.

Many companies who are not direct competitors are willing to allow access and share information, especially if it will be kept confidential. There will often be a need to sign a non-disclosure agreement. Personal contacts and a professional approach play a major part in opening doors; there is usually a need to convince target organisations that mutual benefit will accrue. Potential Benchmarkers should be well briefed and be given sufficient authority to trade sensitive information. Often, a partnership for the exchange of data develops, with reciprocal visits and regular meetings to compare notes.

Independent bodies can be used to gather data from competitive companies, but here it is often only the numbers that can be obtained and not the processes that deliver the numbers.

ANALYSING THE DATA AND IMPLEMENTING IMPROVEMENT

The data from Benchmarking exercises will obviously differ

depending on the activity that has been investigated. However, it should be made up of two elements; what is achieved in terms of numbers (the performance metrics) and how and why it is achieved (the practice). Neither of these is of much use without the other. These two sets of data need to be considered and compared to your current performance in the same area. A further consideration may well be the difficulty of transferring a process that works well in one endeavour into a completely different industry.

The questions are as follows.

- How big is the gap between your performance and theirs?
- How much of their experience is applicable to your situation?

If the data collected during the study is directly comparable, the performance gap is instantly meaningful. Even if your performance is superior there may be things to learn from what others do. The main lessons, though, come from studies which show that your performance is inferior. The question 'Where do we want to be?' can now be answered in detail, with quantified goals based on a knowledge of what the leaders are achieving and how. If the processes, products, company size or business areas are not very similar, then the interpretation of the data will be more difficult and the performance gap may not be as meaningful.

It may also be more difficult to answer 'How do we get from here to there?' What can be done to close the gap? How can the positions be reversed, bearing in mind that your competitors are also making improvements and trying to widen the gap? How far will you go to adopt and adapt new practices? What is involved, how much will it cost and how long will it take? What are the broader implications for the company? These are issues that need to be tackled on a team basis, involving those who really understand the current practices, those with responsibility for steering the future of the company and those with the authority to make the changes.

Once the decision is made to proceed, implementation of the changes must be planned and steered. New targets for the critical activity can be set based on the Benchmark data, and good leadership will be essential to maintain focus and prevent backsliding. Progress towards the new objectives will need to be reviewed regularly and senior management have a key role to play in overseeing and providing support for the whole implementation process.

THE NEXT STEP

Successful companies have taken on board the fact that improvement is a never-ending journey. A commitment to Benchmarking as a driver for continuous improvement means that the implementation of a change to current practices is the end of the beginning, not the beginning of the end. Nothing stands still and as soon as a new practice is established or a Benchmark performance is reached, it may already be out of date. If the activity is still considered to be central to the organisation's existence, it is necessary constantly to review the Benchmark for that activity and repeat the process of looking for best practice wherever it can be found. Xerox call this stage 'recalibrating the Benchmark'.

CASE-STUDY
NCR (MANUFACTURING LTD)

Introduction

When the National Cash Register Company of Dayton, Ohio, USA, now known as NCR, set up in Dundee, they were the first multinational company to move to Scotland after the Second World War.

Operations began at the Camperdown factory in 1946 with the production of the 'Class 100' mechanical cash register which was manufactured there until 1972. In 1961 the company engaged in its first-ever electronic production and, within ten years, small electronic computer systems were in full production, leading the way for electronic point-of-sale terminals, banking terminals, document sorters, computer peripherals, accounting machines and general purpose computer systems.

The first engineering developments took place in 1957 with the design of two new cash registers which were manufactured until the 1970s. Electronic and System Integrated developments followed, creating a strong base for the company's engineering capabilities. NCR has always been ground-breaking in the use of new technologies for the design and manufacture of its products, pioneers in the use of high-density powder metallurgy, rubber to metal bonding, functional and decorative plastic mouldings and ergonomic design, in days when these were unheard of, NCR have always led the way.

Developments such as the encapsulation technique used successfully in No Carbon Required (NCR) paper, Photo Chromic Micro Imaging (PCMI) process and adding to the Century family of computers ran along with the company's development programme of providing more efficient data capturing services. The evolution of Large Scale Integration (LSI) and Metal Oxide Semi-conductor (MOS) circuitry brought about a new range of data terminals for the retail, banking, commerce and industry markets.

The arrival of a new General Manager, James Adamson, coincided with the Research and Development team at the Gourdie, Dundee, factory designing the 1780 Automatic Teller Machine (ATM). In 1980, NCR Dundee was awarded a charter by the NCR Corporate Board in Dayton to design, develop and manufacture ATMs for the World market. NCR is now the market leader in this multimillion pound business, exporting to over 90 countries.

Below, we relate one example from NCR's experience with formal Benchmarking which illustrates the amount of research and effort needed when selecting Benchmarking partners.

Starting To Benchmark

The task of getting the Benchmarking process off the ground was taken on board by Ray S. Robertson, Manager, Operations Programme Management.

Prior to starting the Benchmarking process itself, an initial step was to undertake a thorough research of all the available material on the subject. This established the diverse methods and approaches that could be used at the various stages of the process, the possible problems and pitfalls likely to be encountered, and also a feel for the potential of the methodology for application within NCR.

Having established the ground rules, it was then appropriate to identify the subjects for Benchmarking. NCR have a mission statement called 'Vision and Ten' which incorporates a declaration of purpose, a vision statement and the ten business goals that NCR has set itself. Guidance from this document was supplemented by asking all senior managers and directors what factors they thought were critical to the success of NCR. From these sources, the following list of 20 business measures (metrics) was arrived at:

- Concept to market;
- Shipment performance;
- Product reliability;
- Order-to-ship cycle;
- Manufacturing cycle time;
- Production linearity;
- Inventory (days on hand forward);

- Out-of-box quality;
- Mainline yield;
- On-time supplier delivery;
- Supplier quality, mechanical/electrical;
- Gross margin;
- Return on assets;
- Total value added per production employee;
- Output per square foot;
- Percentage of parts on JIT (*Just In Time*);
- Value of parts on JIT;
- Revenue per employee;
- Inventory accuracy;
- Return on technical investment.

A database was created to store information for each of these categories.

Which Companies To Benchmark Against?

It was decided to set a target of ten companies to Benchmark against and, as a starting point, internal sources were consulted again. Approximately 90 managers and directors were interviewed, and a list of 30 organisations was drawn up. A standard letter was sent to the Managing Director or Chief Executive of all of these companies, enquiring whether they would be interested in a joint Benchmarking exercise with NCR, involving the sharing of performance data and best practices. Only 13 replies were received and out of these 5 were negative, 1 because of overcommitment to other Benchmarking exercises. Furthermore, because two of the companies approached are part of the same organisation, this meant that the list of possible Benchmarking partners was down to 7 from the original list of 30.

The next step was to send to the seven remaining companies a list of the Benchmarking metrics that NCR was interested in pursuing and to establish the performance levels currently being achieved by those companies for each of the metrics. Only one questionnaire was fully completed, but it was felt that sufficient information had been obtained to indicate that visits to all of the companies would be worth while. However, to keep the costs and the time involved within acceptable limits, only four companies were selected for visiting at this stage. One of the four visits, though, showed that first impressions are not always reliable.

Of the three companies not visited as part of this exercise, one had been visited previously on other exercises and demonstrated world-class manufacturing techniques. The second was very receptive to the idea of a visit, but the timing of the enquiry was inconvenient for specific reasons. The third company made a visit to NCR, a good relationship was established and an invitation was made for a reciprocal visit.

However, it was not felt that sufficient useful Benchmarking data could be obtained solely by pursuing the contacts already made and it was decided to cast the net wider.

Identifying The Best Companies In The World

A literature search was carried out to identify the optimum source for a list of the best companies in the world. Many published lists were uncovered and investigated including the *Times 1000, the Electronic Business 200, Japan's Top 50 Companies Turn in a Strong Performance* and *Fortune 500*. From these, the latter was chosen since it gives a large list of companies around the world and is not focused on any specific area of endeavour. It lists the world's largest industrial corporations in terms of sales, profits, assets, stockholders' equity and employees. Within *Fortune 500*, companies are classified into 27 industrial groupings and it was decided to select those 8 groupings with either technology or product similar to NCR.

This gave a total list of 155 companies broken down into the following areas:

Aerospace	16
Computers (including office equipment)	15
Electronics	45
Industrial and farm equipment	28
Motor vehicles and parts	40
Scientific and photographic equipment	7
Toys, sporting goods	1
Transportation equipment	3
Total:	155

The aim has been to analyse and compare the performances of about 100 companies and to select suitable Benchmarking partners from the comparisons made. However, the decision was made to follow up on all 155 organisations; the question was 'How?' The previous activity had already consumed a considerable amount of time and money, the initial response had been poor and the exercise had, to date, yielded insufficient usable material.

For this stage of the investigation, it was decided that a well-designed questionnaire would provide the maximum amount of necessary information, quickly, and at minimum cost. Considerable research, thought and effort was put into designing a suitable questionnaire and a pilot run was carried out on some of the contacts established in the earlier exercise. One of the aims of the design was brevity – so that people would not be discouraged from filling it in. With this in mind, it was decided to reduce the number of metrics being researched. This was achieved by inviting the directors and managers within NCR to revise and prioritise their previous selections. The list was reduced from 20 to the following 13:

- Mainline yield (right-first-time production);
- Product reliability (mean time between failures – in hours);

- Out-of-box quality (simulates customer's perception of quality);
- Concept-to-market (also called 'time to market', measured in weeks);
- Research and development costs versus plan;
- Development schedule versus plan;
- Inventory (days of material on hand);
- Manufacturing cycle time (a measure equitable to responsiveness);
- Revenue growth (to indicate trends);
- Return on assets;
- Return on revenue;
- Revenue per employee;
- Revenue per production employee.

This list of categories, and definitions for each, formed the meat of the questionnaire, with the potential respondent being asked to enter their company's performance data in the space provided beside each metric. Further questions were included to establish the size and type of business, the company's experience of Benchmarking and interest in Benchmarking with NCR, and the respondent's name and position. Considerable space was given to explaining the purpose of the questionnaire, assuring the recipient of NCR's commitment to maintain confidentiality and a promise that all who responded would receive a summary of the findings of the survey. In all, the questionnaire consisted of five, uncrowded, A4 pages.

Locating the address and person to contact for each company proved to be a greater obstacle than had been anticipated. Since most company directories are country-specific, the list of companies had to be classified by country and then the appropriate directory consulted. Only 138 of the original 155 companies were eventually located and the questionnaire was sent out with an explanatory letter to the top person within each organisation.

The response was again disappointing, with 111 companies (80 per cent) not responding at all. Of the other 27, 4 declined to participate for sensitivity reasons, 12 declined because of other commitments and 4 returned only their annual reports. Only 7 companies (5 per cent) responded fully. Research had indicated that between 9 per cent and 15 per cent could have been expected. Perhaps the approach had been made at the wrong level; perhaps the metrics requested were not pursued by some companies; perhaps there were language problems in some cases, since many of the organisations were in countries where English is not the first language.

Analysis

Data from each company were letter-coded to ensure confidentiality and performances were indexed, with the best company (the Benchmark) scoring 100. The indexed values for each company were drawn on to bar graphs for a visual display of the different performance levels within each metric.

No one company did best in all of the metrics and there was a tie for one category:

- Companies A and J came out top for one metric each;
- Company B was the best for two metrics;
- Companies C and E were top in three metrics;
- NCR came top in four of the metrics;
- Companies D, F, G, H, I and K did not come top in any of the metrics.

Since all of the organisations used for the comparison are major companies, it is clear that it is not essential to be number one in every area in order to be successful. Perhaps not surprisingly, all of the companies did well in the out-of-box quality category with there being very little difference between the best and the worst. In other areas, the differences were more marked, sometimes dramatically so. Although the amount of information collected was less than hoped for, it was sufficient for comparisons to be made and to indicate how NCR were placed in the key areas selected.

NCR achieved a Benchmark performance in 4 of the 13 key areas that were selected as being critical to its success. However, they are determined not to get complacent. The comparisons recorded above are quantitative and were made purely by comparing the available numbers. They do not take into account the different industries, the product being made, the processes and the conditions that led to the numbers being generated. (Some of the financial measures, though, are certainly a good guide to the health of any company.)

NCR, of course, have more detail about each of the companies who took part in the study and have made a more detailed qualitative comparison. They are committed to carrying out follow-up investigations into those critical areas where they feel there is room for further improvement. Based on the findings of the study and other data collected, they have identified the companies worth pursuing as Benchmarking partners and have carried out more desk research to discover as much as possible about the companies selected before arranging further visits.

CASE STUDY
THE ROVER GROUP

Introduction

Rover Group is now some five to six years into a Total Quality Management programme and is developing widespread use of the Tools of Quality. Best Practice Benchmarking has been applied as one of a number of delivery mechanisms designed to continue the momentum generated by the first Total Quality Programme.

Various definitions of Benchmarking are available, but one used by Rover Group is: 'a measure of our product, service or practice against our toughest competitors or those companies renowned as industry leaders.'

Rover regard themselves as fortunate in having a close association with Honda who are accepted as a world-class company. However, before the introduction of the Benchmarking process they admit that they were certainly partly guilty of rationalising why the results they observed were not relevant or achievable in their environment.

Rover Group started a Benchmarking programme in early 1990, undertaking literature surveys and seeking out best practice. Support was obtained in this period from the Total Quality consulting group at Rank Xerox Ltd (UK) and it was upon the Rank Xerox case study that the approach within Rover Group was modelled. This was selected because it demonstrated the successful integration of Benchmarking into the overall Total Quality context and the requirements to understand business processes as a prerequisite for success. In a sense it represented a Benchmarking of the Benchmarking process itself!

The collaborative relationship with Honda also emphasised the holistic nature of the business and the clear alignment of activities, and this stimulated a development of the Xerox approach. Rover Body and Pressings were chosen to pilot the Benchmarking process within the Rover Group. This is the business unit with responsibility for body engineering (including the design and development of new products), press tool design and manufacture, body pressings manufacture, and sub-assembly and vehicle body assembly.

The collaborative relationship which the Rover Group enjoys with Honda is regarded as having provided a major asset in undertaking the Benchmarking programme. The collaboration started in 1979 with the Acclaim and advanced significantly in 1990 with Honda taking a 20 per cent holding in the Rover Group and Rover a 20 per cent holding in Honda UK's manufacturing interests. This has been further strengthened with the recent announcement of a number of joint product development programmes and also that of Rover Body and Pressings as a key supplier to Honda UK's manufacturing facility in Swindon.

Learning from Honda

Rover admit that they made many mistakes on their early visits to Honda. They now recognise that if a world-class operation is purely visited without thorough preparation and analysis, then little or no improvement will result. During the 11 years of collaboration many Rover Body and Pressing staff have visited Honda plants. One performance aspect noted was that their changeover times were more than ten times quicker. This was originally talked down on the basis that it was not applicable to Rover's seemingly older equipment. The real truth only emerged recently when a team was established to focus specifically on press line peformance and changeover times. After two months of improvement actions they visited Honda's plants in Japan, and they were surprised that in the majority of cases Honda's equipment was older and less automated than their own. It was the attention to detail which made the difference. They returned with over 2,000 improvement ideas which are now being implemented and a real belief that they could achieve Honda's performance levels as it was not the machinery which would make the difference, but the way it was used.

Rover now believe that they have managed not only to achieve the rate of climb of performance of the Japanese in terms of output and quality, but to achieve what all the best Benchmarking exercises do, that is an improvement on a world-class performance.

Post-Manufacturing Logistics in Rover Body and Pressings

This process devolves into two separate processes, the post-inventory input and the post-inventory output. Post-inventory input, which is considered here, is the activity or process of obtaining material from the manufacturing unit, and filling and controlling the stores.

The objective of Benchmarking the process was to identify world best practice and methods, and also to get the people who 'do the job' involved in the mapping and the identification of the solutions. Without this involvement, commitment and empowerment, only short-term actions and changes to the process will be devised.

A team of the associates who worked in this area was established with representatives from other areas which have either inputs to or outputs from this area. They identified the tasks that they are involved in and from this were coached to create a process flow diagram, and had to identify for themselves the factors which directly affected the measure of customer satisfaction in that area; schedule achievement.

The main reason established for lack of schedule achievement was inadequate inventory control and it was concluded that for this area of the process this would be the key measure of success. In this context, inventory control was defined as the level of accuracy of the control system to the actual number of pallets, part numbers, quantities and locations in the store.

The group then brainstormed all the reasons for problems within inventory accuracy. They then looked outside at a company with world-class levels of inventory accuracy and examined their process. From this analysis and their own brainstorming, actions were identified to implement the changes necessary to improve inventory accuracy.

The success of this Benchmarking exercise was due to the efforts of the team to understand their own operation before their competitive visit. They had already identified some improvements; thus the visit served the purpose of a teambuilding event and a reward for involvement, as well as providing real energy and ideas to move towards world-class performance.

Benchmarking Within Change Management

As a result of Rover Group's experiences of Benchmarking they have realised a need for a sound learning process across Rover Group and as a consequence of this they now have a Change Management Process in which Benchmarking is a key element. This is depicted in Figure 5.1

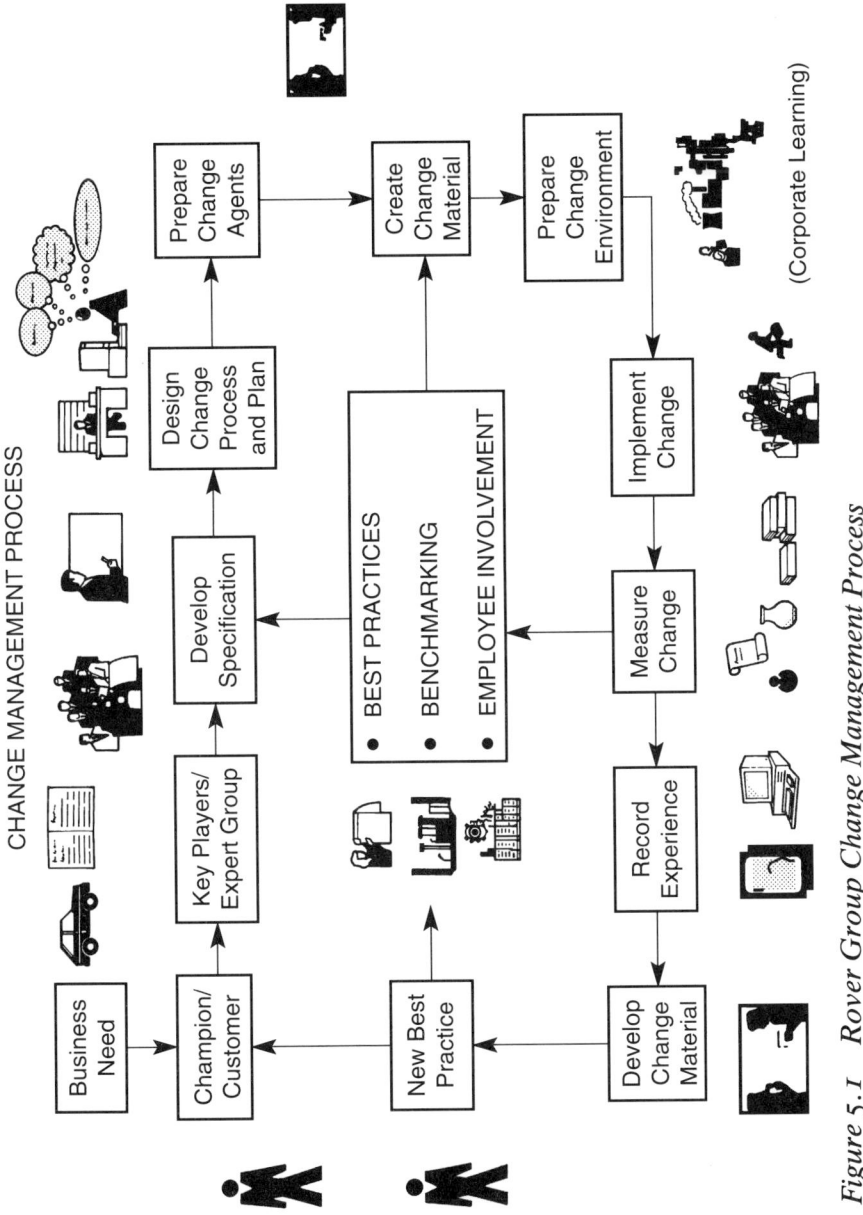

Figure 5.1 Rover Group Change Management Process

6 INTERNAL BENCHMARKING

THE CURRENT POSITION AND THE POTENTIAL FOR INTERNAL BENCHMARKING

In the previous chapter, we defined Internal Benchmarking as essentially the process of making comparisons with other parts of the same organisation. This is a very loose definition, since comparisons could be with other departments, other sites, other companies within the same group (either in the same country or abroad) or between workteams even within the same department. In this chapter we shall explore all of these possibilities. We shall look, in particular, at the potential for exploiting Benchmarking within a group of companies and making comparisons between and within departments, and at mechanisms for Benchmarking of workteam and individual performance.

It is, in many senses, remarkable that such Internal Benchmarking is not already a completely standard way of life. It is hard to believe that Group management do not bring together the experience and best practice within the Group to assist the performance and development of all parts of the Group organisation. Yet it is abundantly clear that in most Western PLCs and Groups that this does not happen. Group structures and the power of the centre tend to vary, but on the whole Group companies tend to be responsible to the centre only for financial performance. As long as targets are met, or performance is not too disastrous, individual local companies are left very much to themselves.

Even if contact exists with the centre, very often individual managers or engineers are not in direct contact with their opposite numbers in other Group locations or factories. The limited contact that does exist takes place on either a formal route or informal route. Formal routes may include annual, six-monthly or quarterly meetings. They tend to have a centrally determined format or agenda, to deal with aspects of performance (outputs) or of central policy (inputs), as well as perhaps attempting to assist in the process of introduction of new technology, or similar.

Informal links arise often because of career movements between corporate sites and tend to provide a means for individual managers to make contact with some source of knowledge or experience about a particular relevant subject. The very informality of these relationships, however, mitigates against a strong analytic approach and represents more the transfer of 'gut feel' based on individual experiences between individuals at various sites, who themselves may be very isolated.

Thus both formal and informal links, which exist within most corporate Groups at present, are not ideal as the exemplars of the Benchmarking principles.

EXPLOITING THE POTENTIAL OF THE GROUP

The Group, however, has enormous potential in this area of sharing best practice, learning from each other both in terms of current practice and bad experiences, providing Benchmarks of performance for group members to aspire to, and providing comparative measures of achievement. For this to happen, however, there does need to be a real belief within the Group that a systematic advantage can be obtained to all participating sites or companies. All too often, attempts at convening such 'Best Practice' Clubs within Groups by the centre, are seen by the operating companies as 'interference from Head Office and the corporate seagulls'. While they are under an obligation to participate in such programmes in order 'to placate Head Office', no real benefit to the site is to be anticipated.

Where, alternatively, the establishment of such 'Self-improvement' clubs arises as a direct result of personnel at various operating companies getting together, this is typically hampered by a concern about lack of interest from Group, or even hostility, and therefore a lack of support from other senior managers at the various sites.

How then, to do it right? The reality is that in many Groups this type of activity has never been planned and policy at the centre is not always clear. Accordingly, one sees short spells of interest by senior central managers leading to the formation or development of such 'clubs', but since there is no established, long-term policy view of their role and the place for Internal Benchmarking, personnel changes and career progression often subsequently bring such programmes to a screeching halt, or a more gradual decline.

One key to doing it right then is planning. An important aspect of this is the development of clear objectives for the Benchmarking activity and a clear view of its priority. The central Board must see the need for the activity, to ensure that best practice spreads more quickly among its various operating companies. This belief in its importance by the central Board, as well as what it can do for the individual companies, must be communicated effectively to the senior management of the operating companies in a way that it becomes a clear priority for their own operation. As always with Benchmarking, however, there is only limited advantage in identifying and evaluating best practice if there is not a clear will, both at the central level and at the operating company level, to then introduce best practice into the other operating sites.

The mechanism for the spread of best practice within the Group is also problematical. Central collection of information tends to be regarded by the operating companies as restrictive, rather than as the basis for enabling transfer of best practice. The threat of central interference, or even sale, has frequently come to the fore in the minds of the managers of the operating companies.

In consequence many Groups, including a number of those operating a 'lean centre' model, have instead concentrated on a central enabling role. A central unit under the direct control of a centre Board director provides, or offers (sometimes on a contract basis), a support service to the operating companies. Here again though, frequently the emphasis is on the provision of the expertise at the centre to the operating companies rather than on the sharing of best practice between the operating companies. This, therefore, frequently results in a feeling in the operating companies that the central function is irrelevant, perhaps staffed with personnel who have insufficient experience of 'the real world' and their actual situation, and that, 'as always', they have to deal with their real problems themselves. In many cases, it has also been true that there is an element of validity in these accusations.

Given the above dangers, clearly the right way forward is a combination of ownership by the operating companies and ownership by the Group centre. To facilitate such ownership and to make the Internal Benchmarking network a reality, champions are needed in each of the operating companies and again in the centre. Drive from the centre is very attractive, but it must be an enlightened drive facilitating the discussion and comparisons between operating companies, rather than prescriptively instituting solutions.

Clearly, in a large Group, it will not be possible to identify champions and make Benchmarking a clear priority simultaneously in all the operating companies, nor probably would this be desirable. Some companies will have more immediate time- and energy-consuming activities that they must complete; such as introducing a new technology, obtaining certification to

ISO 9000/BS 5750 etc. In most cases, operating companies will be self-selecting, although subject to the encouragement of the champion at the centre. This may well mean that the best companies in the Group, the ones that potentially have least to gain from Benchmarking with other Group companies, will be the first to sign up. While from a steady-state perspective this seems far from ideal, in reality it does provide probably the best basis for the Internal Benchmarking 'Club' to get off the ground, since the people involved will be the most informed, the most motivated and from the companies best able to take the long-term view. The 'Club' will therefore be in its best position to survive the initial problems of start-up, to get round management indifference or hostility, to survive changes in personnel at the centre and in the operating companies, or even changes of corporate policy. With this strength, facilitated by the corporate champion, new member sites or operating companies can be introduced into and absorbed into the 'Club' activities.

To begin with such activities may be relatively simple; meetings held at each other's sites, with presentations of local approaches and performance, as well as, perhaps, workshop sessions on fundamental concerns across Group companies. This can form the basis for individual or small group Benchmarking partnerships between member companies. The whole 'Club' may develop a Benchmarking Grid, and set up crucial measures against which to measure themselves and each other. As time passes, the Club as a whole may begin to engage in collective External Benchmarking, selecting world best practice companies outside their Group for comparison. Again, the pooled resources thus available and the collective weight of the consortium may facilitate such External Benchmarking, when it might be prohibitive for an individual member company.

The organisation of such a 'Club' typically requires some resources and a 'secretariat'. Very frequently these are provided by the centre. If, as in some Groups, there is a management consultancy, research or training facility in the Group which is itself run as an operating company, then this may play host at least part of the time to the Group and provide the secretariat, possibly on a straightforward membership fee basis. The Group-wide 'Club' concept has many advantages over the one-off service from a central facility and also over the concept of participation in external multiorganisation clubs. Continuity is provided, with a reduction in the problems of commercial confidentiality, to some extent shared circumstances and reinforcement of some already existing personal relationships.

MECHANISMS FOR INTER- AND INTRADEPARTMENTAL COMPARISONS

The same advantages which exist for Internal Benchmarking of operating companies within the Group also apply for Inter-Departmental Benchmarking and even comparisions within a department. Different departments may possess similar functional activities, or business processes, or may have common aspects of work organisation or personnel matters. For example, each department may have to work out its holiday rota, deal with its interdepartmental and external mail each morning, organise its own secretarial work and handle incoming messages when relevant staff are not available. Benchmarking of these working practices, organisational issues and the corresponding successful performance against other departments can be highly beneficial, leading to the spread of best practice identified in one part of the organisation to other operating departments.

It is interesting that this aspect of Internal Benchmarking has really been labelled as a Benchmarking activity, despite its clear similarity to the processes described in the previous section.

The spreading of good practice from one department to another is in fact a very problematic area. In most organisations the 'not invented here syndrome', together with interdepartmental communication barriers, means that such good practice is unlikely to spread, unless identified at a sufficiently senior level of management and consciously legislated for, or encouraged, throughout more departments.

For organisations pursuing quality improvement or Total Quality Management (TQM) programmes, a further complication is the need to balance local involvement, identification and development of solutions, with the need to spread good practice as quickly as possible to obtain the greatest benefit. In the real world, many TQM programmes are particulary deficient in this respect, since the spreading of good practice identified at a local level has not been clearly thought through. Clearly, to be consistent with the objectives of TQM, each local area needs to evaluate the worth and transferability of the 'superior' practice developed elsewhere, decide positively to pursue its introduction and gain clear ownership of its implementation. This is in contrast to central management legislating for its introduction and is completely consistent with the concept of Benchmarking.

Typically, the same problems which exist at the Group level of Benchmarking exist also at the interdepartmental level. In particular, the role of central management *vis-à-vis* departmental management is crucial, the primary need being for a facilitation role, with the ownership of the process of searching for better practice being with the local departmental management. Central management can be key in getting departments, or departmental representatives, together in exactly the same way as corporate management may do for Group operating companies.

There are, however, advantages at this interdepartmental level compared to that at Group level. Typically, central management is much more in control. Communication between departments, however bad, is better, as is communication with central management. Staff are much more likely to know each other and already to have to work together in certain respects. Perhaps more importantly, the whole of the TQM programme is concentrating on involving and communicating with everyone, and staff are participating not just within their departments but across departmental boundaries. Thus the culture is appropriate to this particular Internal Benchmarking process. In addition, the Steering Group of senior management heading up the site TQM programme, as well as the facilitators supporting the programme, are in an excellent position to identify good practice, and encourage its investigation and transfer.

Unfortunately, since most TQM programmes focus in greatest detail at the site or operating company level rather than at Group level, there is no analogue of these mechanisms at the level of Group Benchmarking.

How a department sets about Benchmarking itself against others varies between companies, largely according to the nature of the TQM programme introduced. Where, as in most successful programmes, a strong responsibility for quality improvement is placed on departmental management early, so that there is not a separation into quality and 'real work', then typically part of the department's planning will specifically identify opportunities for improvement from learning from other departments. Included in this will be the straightforward transfer of practices, as well as the broader use of information from other departments to solve local problems. The important message here is that for this type of activity to be successful there must be in place a coherent approach to departmental improvement, as well as the interfunctional, interdepartmental improvement teams which are often highlighted, perhaps too greatly, within TQM programmes.

All that has been said at the interdepartmental level can be repeated at lower levels within departments. Ultimately, successful workteams or Quality Circles can Benchmark aspects of their activities against those of others. Indeed, it is noteworthy that many successful Quality Circle programmes do encourage healthy competition between 'competing' circles and that this in itself provides a lot of motivation.

BENCHMARKING JOB COMPETENCIES: BOC SPECIAL GASES CASE STUDY

Introduction

BOC's Special Gases is part of BOC Limited and a subsidiary of the BOC Group. It sells small volume specialist gases and gas mixtures. It has a wide customer base in the UK and overseas, with 20,000 products and 15,000 customers. About 2,000 new products are introduced each year and about 1,000 disappear. Over the last ten years it can be described as having moved from a 'jobbing environment' to becoming much more process oriented. It has had an 11 per cent compound annual growth rate and did at one time suffer from approximately 20 per cent staff turnover each year. A major stimulus for change has come from business expansion which, together with site limitations, has required the investment in a new site at Immingham.

The Immingham site in South Humberside represents a £25 million site investment and is a high-tech facility with a responsibility to service a wide customer base, including semiconductor manufacturers, and the desire to focus on quality and customer service. Accordingly, a new human resource strategy was developed to support the business strategy and to provide a blueprint or Benchmark for the UK operations.

Benchmarking at BOC Special Gases

Within the BOC Group, Internal Benchmarking exists in terms

of financial data with comparisons from country to country, but this is regarded as of only limited assistance to identify improvement areas. A desire existed to Benchmark processes and in Benchmarking against other parts of the corporation it was revealed that Special Gases were focusing too much on a day-to-day basis and, in particular, were not addressing the people issues. Communication and morale were identified as key areas for improvement.

Benchmarking within the Group on broad financial measures against similar units, leads to probes of the deficiencies and the introduction of improvement efforts. Annual formal meetings take the place of international panels, made up of senior management, once a year and these result in the setting up of action teams. An example is the Just-In-Time approach where BOC Special Gases is leading the Group. Another example is in the use of international design teams, for example for the new facility at Immingham. As well as formal processes, informal networking also occurs.

At a Group level, Benchmarking also takes place against competitors, although obtaining competitor data has proved difficult, except for the use of very detailed market research data. On safety, BOC Special Gases compares against Du Pont, who they see as the best in class.

Job Competencies At Immingham

At the new Immingham site, 16 performance indicators are now in place which are summed to give an overall site 'quality index'. The intention is to 'roll out' these measures to the other sites. The key is seen as competency analysis and self-managing workteams. Job competencies are the unifier, with the intention being to look at successful individuals to find out why they are successful, and to transfer this success to other individuals and teams.

Behind the BOC Special Gases approach is the belief that

'people are the source of our strength'. Each employee can affect the success of the business; all are involved to participate to the best of their ability. Each contributes to Special Gases' reputation, and vitality and involvement in teamwork are the core human values.

In order to provide the Benchmark for future people and management activities, and to develop a selection process for the new jobs created at the Immingham site, consultants were used to undertake analysis of staff competencies at the Crawley and Morden sites, and to prepare a job competency model for Immingham. The aim was to determine the strengths, to isolate weaknesses and provide critical data for manpower planning at the new site. In this sense, it was about Benchmarking the future site against the present sites and, in turn, using the people management activities at the new Immingham site as a Benchmark for future people management across BOC Special Gases.

Since Immingham is the most technically developed site to date, the jobs at Immingham are not the same as at existing sites and involve multiskilling and self-supervision. Thus, direct isolation and Benchmarking of core competencies was not appropriate and the results of the research into job competencies carried out initially with staff in similar positions at Crawley and Morden were reviewed in a management workshop to define the new competencies requirements.

The aim was to identify what behaviour supports superior performance and what behaviours really make the difference. Initial behavioural event interviews with appropriate employees were followed by job competency analysis. The individuals interviewed were also categorised into those with superior performance and those who were average, with poor performers not being interviewed. A distinction was made between distinguishing competencies which differentiated the superior performers from the average (in which they were significantly less prevalent) and threshold competencies that are important characteristics for the job, but make no difference between good and superior performance.

A competency is defined as any knowledge, skill, behaviour, motive or thought pattern that is frequently and consistently used in a job. In focusing on competencies we are identifying the individuals who are successful, establishing what they do that makes them successful, establishing precisely how and why they do what they do, and focusing on their behaviour. Interviewees were asked to identify the most critical situations which they encounter in the work they do and then describe these in considerable detail, including what led to the situation, who was involved, what the interviewee wanted to accomplish, what was accomplished and the outcome of the incident. From this competencies were identified and analysed.

A total of 17 competencies were identified and these were seen as falling together into 5 clusters. This overall competency model is shown, together with the percentage figure showing the overall incidence for each competency, throughout the study in Figure 6.1.

Competency requirements are clearly different for each job. For example, gas fillers dealing with highly toxic or flammable products and often working alone (type III fillers) will have to be constantly aware of these facts and adopt an approach that may not be necessary in other types of filling jobs (type I/II). Thus competency models were generated for each job type and competencies were combined to represent new generic jobs at Immingham; for example, where a filling and analysis job was combined.

About half of the sample interviewed were supervisors and these jobs carried different and additional competency requirements. Instances of a supervisory nature in the interview were therefore coded separately, in order to isolate competence associated with that role. This also had the benefit of providing a 'pure' model of job competence and giving an insight into the special requirements of the self-supervising environment at Immingham.

Figure 6.2 contrasts, for each job type and supervisors generally, those competencies that were most frequently demonstrated. Figure 6.3 shows the mean incidences of actual frequencies of competencies for each job type.

Where a competency is frequently demonstrated, there is strong evidence to suggest that it is a basic or 'threshold' requirement for that job. Among these there will be a small number of 'distinguishing competencies' that superior performers do more often, in more situations, with better results than average performers.

For filling jobs there appears to be a total of nine competencies that are, at least in part, able to distinguish performance. Distinguishing competencies differ between type III and types I/II fillers as shown in Figures 6.4 and 6.5(a) and (b).

The above competency analysis provides a Benchmark for Immingham, since it shows the current competencies of employees at two other sites. However, competency requirements at Immingham will not be the same as at those sites, partly due to new jobs at Immingham requiring an amalgam of competencies between two or more jobs, and because of cultural and technological differences between those sites and Immingham. While it is believed that there are unlikely to be competencies needed at Immingham that have been excluded from the analysis, the analysis identified weaknesses in employee behaviour at Crawley and Morden which are believed to be crucial to the new requirements at Immingham. Weaknesses identified included a poor customer orientation and that team skills are infrequently used at present, and these were regarded as being a priority area for work organisation at Immingham.

Accordingly a workshop was used to identify specific Immingham requirements, taking into account the working practices and environments which will apply. The outcome of

THE COMPETENCY MODEL

Competency model
and representation
of each competency

Competency	Representation in Model
Influence	4.8%
Production Orientation (Targets)	5.5%
Communication	13.3%
Seeks Information	9.8%
Standards (Takes Care)	11.8%
Flexible / Commitment	7.0%
Customer Orientation	2.0%
Work Planning (Efficiency)	12.5%
Knowledge and Experience	9.0%
Coaching	5.8%
Team / Other Orientation	1.5%
Alert	7.5%
Safety Conscious	3.8%
Calm	1.3%
Independent	0.8%
Mental Imagery	2.5%
Cognitive	1.3%

BOC
SPECIAL
GASES

Figure 6.1   The Competency Model

COMPETENCIES

Most frequently observed Competencies in each job

Competency	Cylinder Prep	Type I/II	Type III	Lab	Admin	Supv	Driver
Influence						•	
Production Orient	•			•	•	•	•
Communication			•	•	•	•	•
Seeks Information				•	•	•	•
Standards (Care)	•	•	•	•		•	•
Flexible	•	•		•	•	•	•
Customer Orient					•		•
Work Planning	•	•	•	•	•	•	•
Experience	•	•	•	•	•	•	•
Coaching			•		•	•	
Team / Other Orient			•		•		
Alert		•	•			•	•
Safety Conscious			•			•	
Independent			•				
Mental Imagery			•				
Cognitive							

BOC SPECIAL GASES

Figure 6.2   Competencies: I

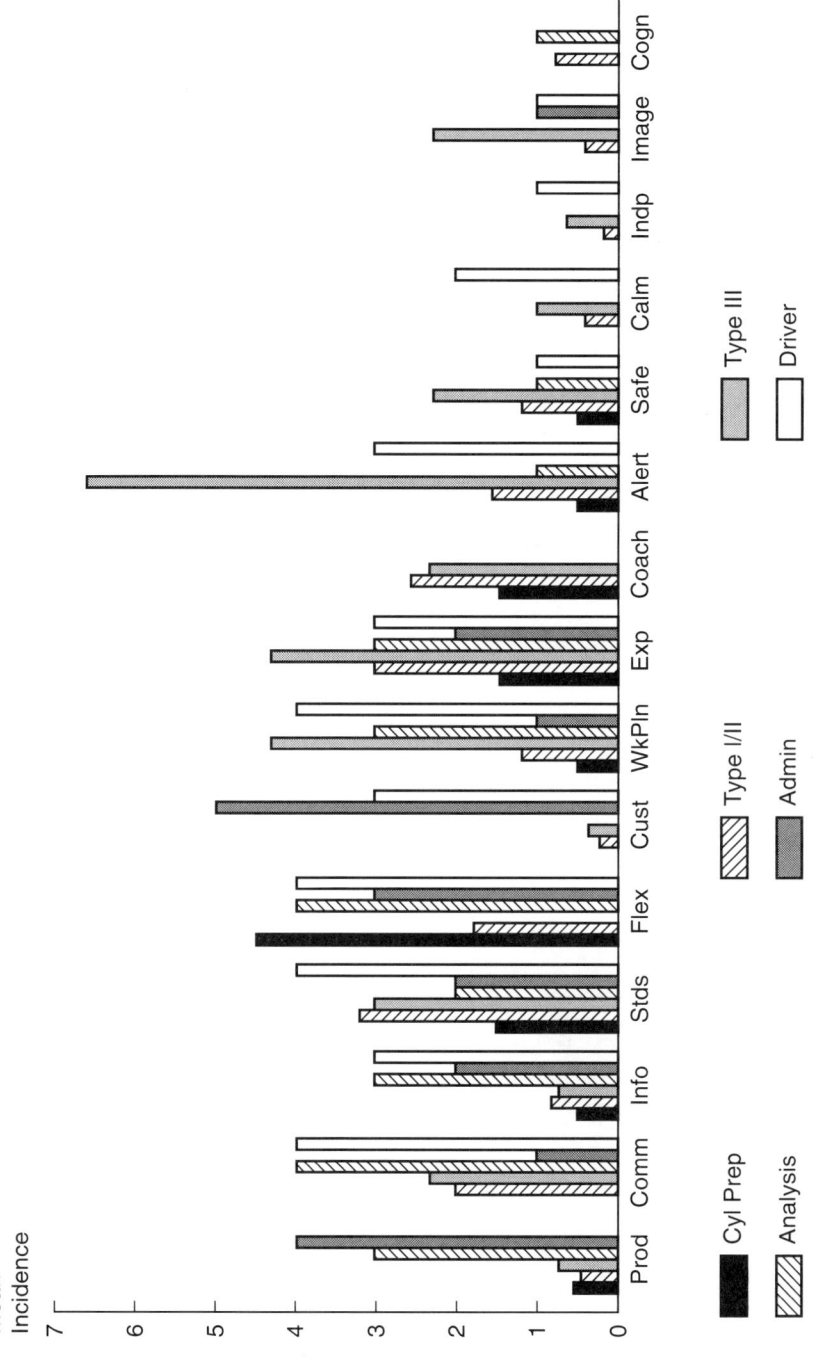

Figure 6.3   Comparison of jobs – job incidents only

COMPETENCIES

Example of Distinguishing Competencies of Cylinder filling positions

N.B. The Symbol (●) indicates that these competencies are only slightly more prevalent in superior performers

Competency	Type I/II	Type III	All Fillers
Communication	●	●	●
Seeks Information	⊙		⊙
Standards (Takes Care)	●		●
Flexible / Commitment	●		
Work Planning (Efficiency)	⊙	● ⊙ ●	⊙
Knowledge and Experience	●		⊙
Coaching			
Mental Imagery	⊙	⊙	
Cognitive			

BOC
SPECIAL GASES

Figure 6.4   Competencies: 2

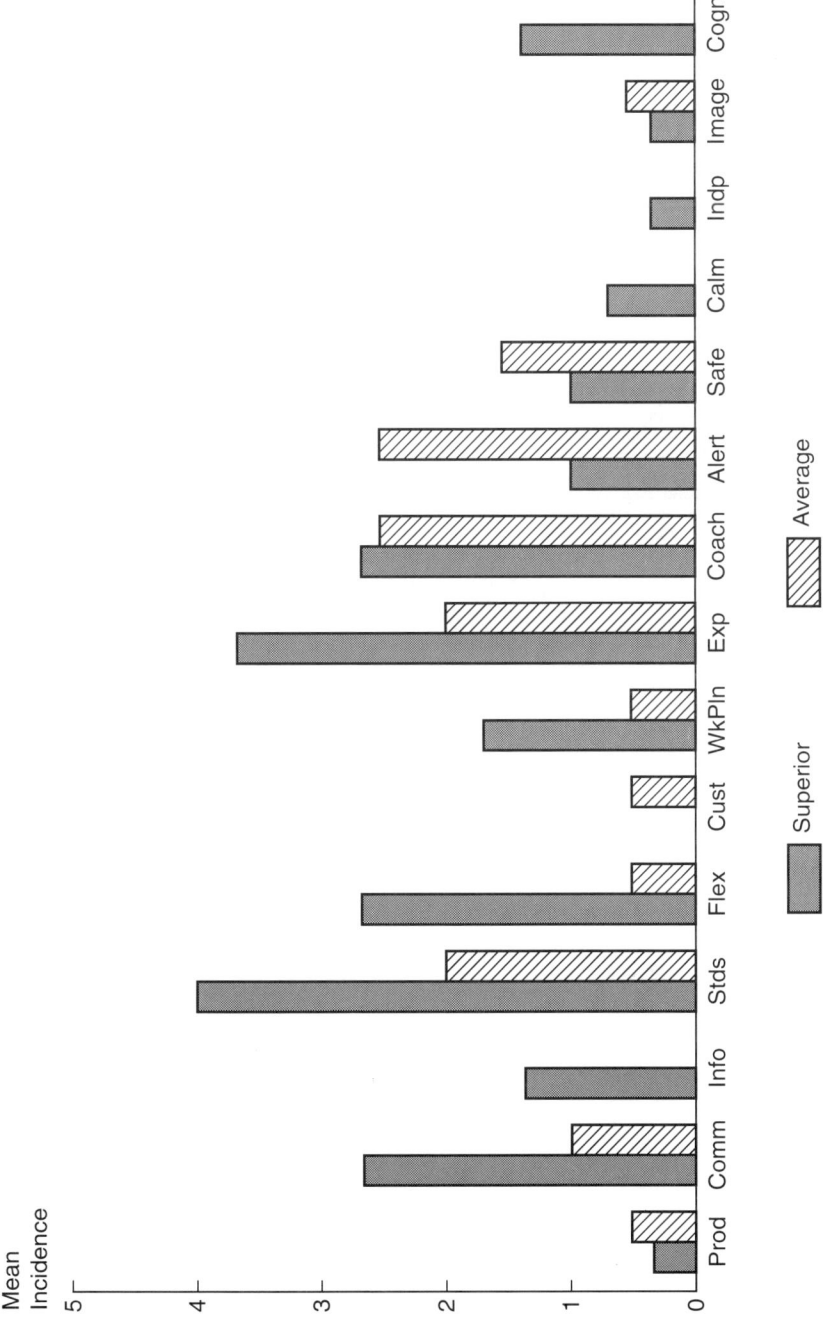

Figure 6.5(a)   Type I/II job incidents only

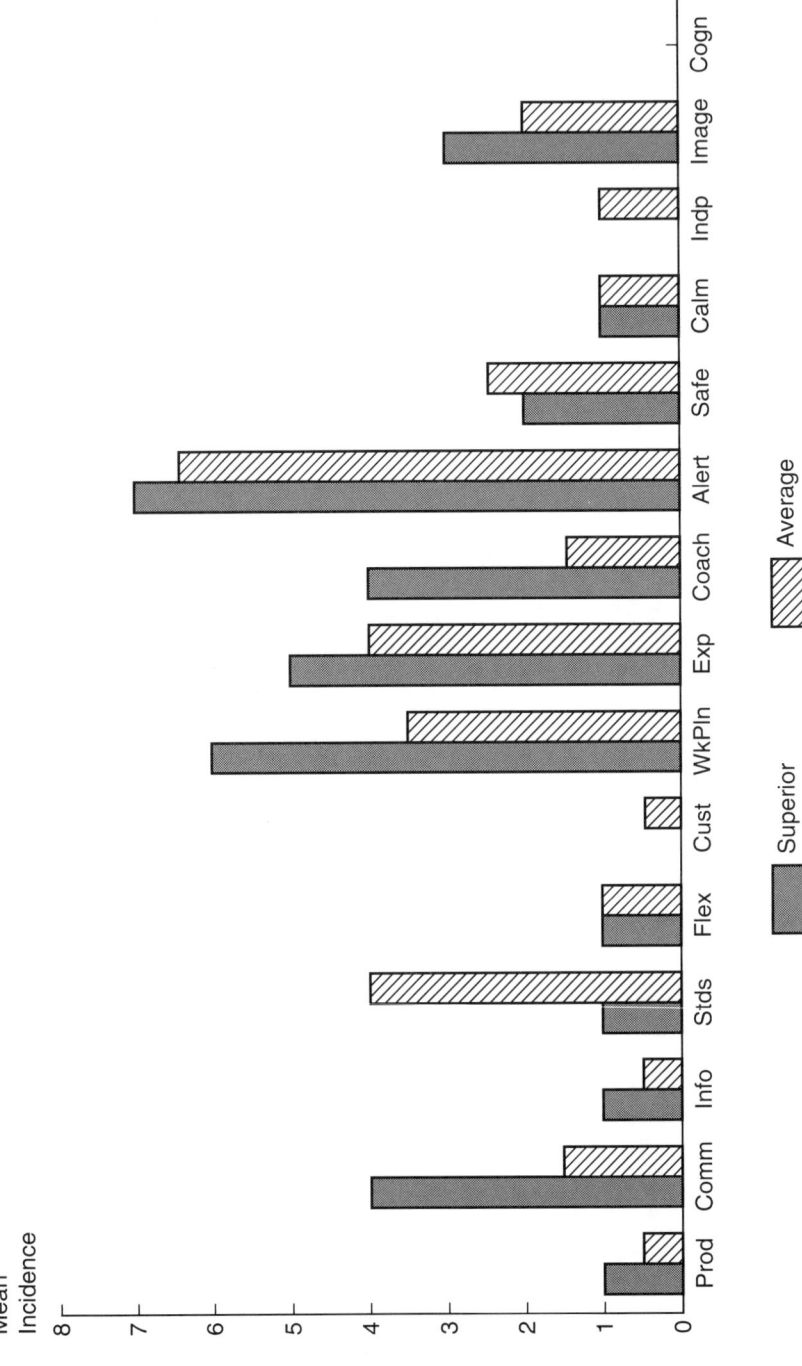

Figure 6.5(b)   Type III

this workshop was to identify the competencies which formed the basis of the recruitment process to be used at Immingham. Core competencies required for all jobs were divided into two groups to be assessed at first and second interview. In addition, competencies unique to the type III filling jobs were also identified. These are depicted in Figure 6.6. As an illustration of how this is used in the interview process, Figures 6.7(a) and (b) show the type of behavioural evidence which is sought to support the core competence of planning and flexibility. Interviewing for competence, then, was in two distinct phases in order to allow the provision of an opportunity to display behaviour sought through case studies and exercises, and the provision of real examples from their own work history. Past behaviour is taken as significant in predicting future behaviour and candidates were scored during the interview process. On this basis, out of a total of 1,427 applicants, 30 were initially recruited; representing a ratio of 47 applicants to 1 placement. The average interview length was one-and-a-half hours.

To validate the process it is necessary to correlate behavioural event interview scores against individual performance. The appraisal process focuses on both measurable indicators and observed behaviours. The employee opinion survey that took place in 1993 provided data and the results will be used to Benchmark superior performance across BOC Special Gases.

BOC Special Gases and the European Quality Award

The European Quality Award is discussed in some detail in Chapter 10, together with other award criteria that can be used as Benchmarks of world performance.

In 1992 the European Quality Award and various associated prizes were awarded for the first time. The award winner was Rank Xerox, but BOC Special Gases, together with Milliken and Ubisa, were prize winners. Many of the award criteria are

1. **Core Competencies to be assessed at first interview**

   - PLANNING   As described in the original model.

   - FLEXIBLE   This is a combination of 'Flexible' in the original model, together with the ability to learn.

   - QUALITY   This is a combination of 'Standards';
     CONSCIOUS   'Customer Orientation'; and 'Safety Conscious'.

   - TRANSFER OF   This is a combination of 'Communication'
     INFORMATION   and 'Seeks Information'.

2. **Competencies for second stage interview**

   - PRODUCTION   As described in the original model.
     ORIENTATION

   - TEAMWORKING   A development of the original competency 'Team/Other Orientation' to reflect the working practices at Immingham.

3. **Type III Competencies**

   - MENTAL   As described in the original model.
     IMAGERY

   - ALERT   As described in the original model.

Figure 6.6   Competencies

about people; employees, customers and members of society. Concentrating on the people, their needs and competencies, together with the competency requirement of jobs has been a major part of BOC Special Gases' people-centred approach, which is to 'match as far as possible our business and people plan with our employees' needs and expectations'.

Benchmarking of individual, job and site competencies has been used to find the right people for the job, and will be used in the future for performance appraisal, training and development, succession planning, and recruitment and selection.

> ## CORE COMPETENCY
> ## - *PLANNING*

Evidence sought:
- Making best use of own and other people's time
- Planning work so that tasks are undertaken concurrently
- Concerned to be efficient
- Thinks ahead and is prepared for events that will change plans

BOC
SPECIAL
GASES

Figure 6.7(a)   Core competencies: planning

> ## CORE COMPETENCY
> ## - *FLEXIBILITY*

Evidence sought:
- Enthusiasm for a challenge
- Openness to change and novel situations
- Commitment
- Keenness to learn new skills/jobs
- Acceptance of change

BOC
SPECIAL
GASES

Figure 6.7(b)   Core competency: flexibility

7 EXTERNAL BENCHMARKING AND HOW TO DO IT

INTRODUCTION

In Chapter 5 we discussed the nature of the Benchmarking process and Internal Benchmarking in particular was explored further in Chapter 6. This chapter focuses in more detail on External Benchmarking. It provides an overview of how many companies have implemented External Benchmarking; how to do it right and how not to do it wrong.

ORGANISATION STRUCTURE AND RESPONSIBILITIES

The 1991 survey by the International Benchmarking Clearing House revealed that 62 per cent of the sample of companies investigated did not 'yet' have a formal Benchmarking department or staff. Of the small number of organisations that do have recognised Benchmarking departments or staff, 52 per cent have Benchmarking contained within the Quality Department or organisation. Sixteen per cent have Benchmarking reporting directly to top management, 4 per cent to Strategic Planning and 4 per cent to Marketing. It is no surprise, given the approach of this book, to find Benchmarking activities so integrated into Quality programmes.

In those organisations not having a Benchmarking department as such, 83 per cent report that it is the Quality department which is responsible for Benchmarking co-ordination. Such departments include Total Quality Management (TQM) departments, Quality Assurance departments or Corporate Quality departments. Exceptionally, Benchmarking is the direct responsibility of market research, organisational development or management analysis.

At the current time such Benchmarking 'departments' or staff groups are not only thin on the ground across companies, but they are also rather 'thin' within the companies. The above survey indicated that the number of full-time staff varied from 0 to 17, and the number of part-time staff from 1 to 20. However, 32 per cent had only one full-time or part-time staff member. Clearly, additional assistance would be necessary for major Benchmarking activities.

Since Benchmarking is a new area of business activity, it is yet to be formalised in many organisational structures or job descriptions. In the survey, two-thirds affirm that Benchmarking responsibilities were incorporated into few or almost no job descriptions and 84 per cent said that Benchmarking was incorporated into few or almost no performance appraisals within their organisation. Clearly, it would be appropriate for an organisation which takes Benchmarking seriously to incorporate the explicit recognition of Benchmarking activities into job descriptions and performance appraisals. One must assume that this has yet to develop in the majority of the organisations surveyed, because of their relatively short experience of undertaking it.

Since 80 per cent of the companies surveyed had been conducting Benchmarking studies for less than five years, this lack of institutionalisation of Benchmarking activities is no particular surprise, but it is also reflected in the lack of a clear, unambiguous role of Benchmarking staff. In the survey 30 per cent saw themselves as managers or co-ordinators of activities, while 27 per cent saw themselves as champions or leaders, 16 per cent as facilitators, consultants or trainers, 11 per cent as initiators or developers, and 3 per cent as process owners.

SUPPORT FOR BENCHMARKING ACTIVITIES

One aspect of support is, of course, top management commitment, and the identification of mechanisms for encouraging such commitment and developing champions in top management is, in many organisations, a necessity if meaningful activities are to take place. Strategies vary as to how such support is engendered and encouraged, but typically education and awareness are top of the list.

As well as top management commitment, other internal support facilities to enable Benchmarking may take the form of the establishment of Benchmarking libraries, the establishment of guides for Benchmarking practices, the setting up of databases, the development of standard confidentiality agreements and guidelines etc. In Figure 7.1 we show the incidence of the use of various support mechanisms from the International Benchmarking Clearing House survey. Interestingly, 57 per cent have developed introductory Benchmarking classes and training for Benchmarking participants, while 46 per cent have established a Benchmarking library for secondary research. One-third of the sample have created practice guides, databases, confidentiality agreements, legal guidelines and a Benchmarking code of ethics. Smaller percentages have written Benchmarking mission statements or handbooks for managers.

Since business processes form the basis for much Benchmarking activity, a list of processes for the company or industry is likely to be a particularly useful supporting resource. Approximately a quarter of the companies in the survey indicated that they have such a list.

While 46 per cent of the sample indicated that their company had developed a Benchmarking library, it should be remem-

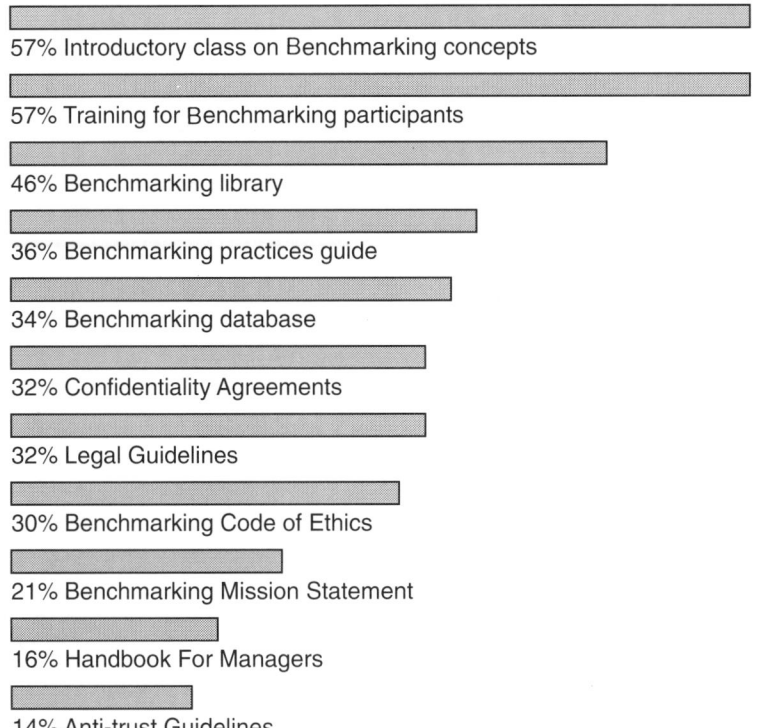

57% Introductory class on Benchmarking concepts

57% Training for Benchmarking participants

46% Benchmarking library

36% Benchmarking practices guide

34% Benchmarking database

32% Confidentiality Agreements

32% Legal Guidelines

30% Benchmarking Code of Ethics

21% Benchmarking Mission Statement

16% Handbook For Managers

14% Anti-trust Guidelines

Source: 'Studying Industries' Benchmarking Practices', American Productivity and Quality Centre, 1992.

Figure 7.1   Benchmarking support (N = 44)

bered that other general company library facilities may be important in the Benchmarking process, provided they are adequately resourced and, preferably, that librarians are adequately trained about Benchmarking activities.

In a similar way, as well as Internal Benchmarking databases within the company, about half of the sample reported using outside databases, possibly gaining access through their company library. Diverse databases are typically used, but most commonly, respondents in the survey indicated using a number of the Dialog databases, including ABI inform, Compendex and PTS Promt. In addition, Lexis/Nexis, Dun and Bradstreet, Datatimes and trade assocation databases were sometimes mentioned, and these would also be good sources.

Other support for Benchmarking activities comes from the use of consultants and membership of various supporting organisations such as Benchmarking Networks. While such networks are only just developing in the UK and Europe, and are often themselves only just finding their feet and learning how to work effectively as networking organisations, in the US there has been a longer history and about half the organisations in the survey reported that they were members of organisations or associations which support Benchmarking efforts. Fifty-six per cent of the sample were using outside consultants.

BENCHMARKING TEAMS

The great majority of companies use a team approach to Benchmarking. In the US survey 94 per cent report using a team approach to Benchmarking and only 19 per cent view poor teamwork as a major reason why Benchmarking studies are unsuccessful.

Getting the correct team to undertake Benchmarking activities, however, is crucial. In the survey 63 per cent reported including facilitators on their Benchmarking teams and nearly half believed that the use of facilitators is important to Benchmarking study success. Fifty-five per cent used staff Benchmarking consultants, while some 11 per cent used external consultants as team participants (see Figure 7.2).

Very often process owners are chosen as team members and experience suggests that lack of process owner involvement is an important factor contributing to unsuccessful studies and implementations. Various other stakeholders should also be included, including process customers, suppliers and representatives from relevant departments. Most frequently, team members are selected for their process knowledge or expertise, but it may also be due to their interest in Benchmarking, their availability to participate, technical or communication skills, or

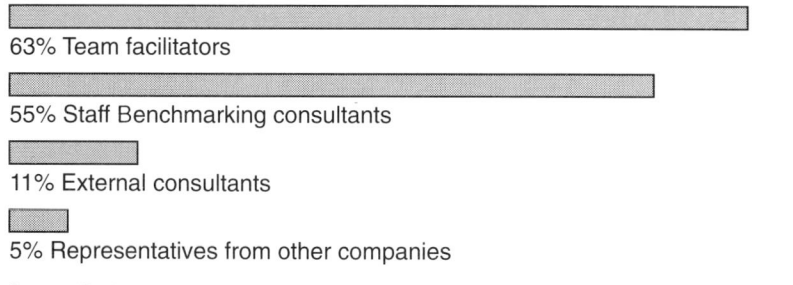

63% Team facilitators

55% Staff Benchmarking consultants

11% External consultants

5% Representatives from other companies

Source: 'Studying Industries' Benchmarking Practices', American Productivity and Quality Centre, 1992.

Figure 7.2   Members commonly included on teams (N = 38)

authority to implement change.

In most cases, it is the process owner who is assigned the responsibility for team selection. Selection criteria vary between applications and at the current time do not appear to be standardised within most organisations.

Team size also varies and, as in other areas of improvement, the team should be large enough to ensure adequate representation and the accomplishment of the task in hand, while being small enough to allow for the co-ordination of team efforts. In the American survey, the vast majority of the sample (81 per cent) typically assembled teams ranging from 4 to 8 members, while 56 per cent reported teams of 4 to 5 members, and 25 per cent had 6 to 8 members. Sub-teams are also sometimes used.

Freeing up adequate time for Benchmarking team members to participate in the Benchmarking activities is another crucial aspect of successful Benchmarking. The American survey reveals that approximately half of the companies sampled indicated that team members typically spend 10 to 25 per cent of their time on Benchmarking-related activities, with a quarter of the sample saying they spend less than 10 per cent of their time and just under a quarter of the sample saying they spend more than 25 per cent of their time. The level of time commitment will also fluctuate during the various stages of the Benchmarking process.

BENCHMARKING STUDIES

The initiation of Benchmarking projects within companies varies considerably. In the International Benchmarking Clearing House study, 36 per cent reported that process owners most commonly launched studies, while 30 per cent designate middle management as the initiators. Interestingly, only 6 per cent report that top management initiate studies and only 4 per cent that Benchmarking staff do this. In other companies, process owners, together with top or middle management, jointly initiate the Benchmarking activities.

Management of Benchmarking studies, however, is most typically with middle management (52 per cent in the study), while in many companies it varies greatly from study to study. Senior management and process owners appear to be only very infrequently involved in Benchmarking study management.

Another crucial issue for companies going down the Benchmarking route must be how much all this is going to cost. Unfortunately this is an area where data are extremely sparse with most organisations appearing to operate on a somewhat marginal costing basis. Indeed, in the American study, only 27 per cent reported that budgets had been developed for Benchmarking studies and few respondents were able to esti- mate the cost for a typical Benchmarking study. In fact only seven did, with study costs ranging from $20,000 to $250,000 with most in the vicinity of $40 – 50,000.

If the activity is not costed, it is hard to undertake a cost- benefit analysis and to provide a justification in financial terms for the activity. Thirty-eight per cent of the American sample almost always, or usually, undertake such a cost-benefit analysis, with a further 19 per cent sometimes doing this. Good practice would say it should always be done, but the fact that it is not at least indicates that the degree of belief in the activity must be high. Nevertheless, senior management are likely to want to know the payback, however difficult it is to estimate, and it can be good internal politics for Benchmarking to be able to provide such information.

Another requirement for the organisation wishing to undertake Benchmarking activities is some concept of the time requirement to complete the study. Clearly, there is no simple answer to this, since it will depend critically on the processes being investigated and local conditions in the organisation, as well as on experience of Benchmarking – as you learn you get better at doing it. However, the American survey indicated the typical lengths of Benchmarking studies in Figure 7.3. This indicates that about 30 per cent of studies take under 2 months, while 52 per cent take between 2 and 6 months, and 17 per cent take 6 months to a year.

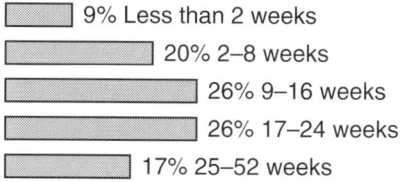

9% Less than 2 weeks
20% 2–8 weeks
26% 9–16 weeks
26% 17–24 weeks
17% 25–52 weeks

Source: 'Studying Industries' Benchmarking Practices', American Productivity and Quality Centre, 1992.

Figure 7.3   Length of typical Benchmarking study (N = 46)

One particularly problematic area for new starters in Benchmarking is the selection of Benchmarking partners. Common practice, as vindicated by the American study, is that the performance level of the company concerned, or the perception that that company is best in class, is most often regarded as critical in selection of study partners. In the American study 64 per cent of survey participants identified this factor, while 50 per cent identified a willingness of a recipient company to partner or share, 32 per cent identified their potential credibility or reputation of a partner, 23 per cent pointed to similar processes, 18 per cent identified the same industry or similar business, and 11 per cent pointed to the location. It is also interesting that 28 per cent of the survey reported that they have refused a request to be Benchmarked, most frequently because of problems of competitiveness or proprietory value, because the requestor was inadequately prepared or because there was no perceived benefit.

The conduct of Benchmarking site visits is one of some subtlety, where many naïve, new starting companies mistakenly go for 'a general look around', rather than having a prepared plan showing clear targets of what they hope to achieve from the visit. In the American study, a clear statement of objectives, purpose or need was identified by the participants as the most important requirement for site visits in most cases. Also interestingly, while 31 per cent reported that typically only 1 process is Benchmarked, 38 per cent reported that in a typical study 3 to 5 processes would be Benchmarked. Site visits are used by the majority (54 per cent) as a data-gathering tool in almost all, or in most, studies. Fifty-two per cent of respondents visit 2 to 3 companies for each study conducted, while 21 per cent are visiting 4 to 5 companies per study.

Apart from site visits, other data collection methods are a central aspect for the Benchmarking process. Figure 7.4 shows the extent of use of various data-gathering methods by the respondents in the American Study.

In undertaking Benchmarking it is normal to develop or adapt some form of Benchmarking process model with clearly identified steps for the Benchmarking activity. More than 80 per cent of the American study report doing this and the International Benchmarking Clearing House itself utilises a four-step model: 1 plan, 2 collect, 3 analyse and 4 improve. Models used by the various companies vary greatly in the number of steps identified, ranging in the International Benchmarking

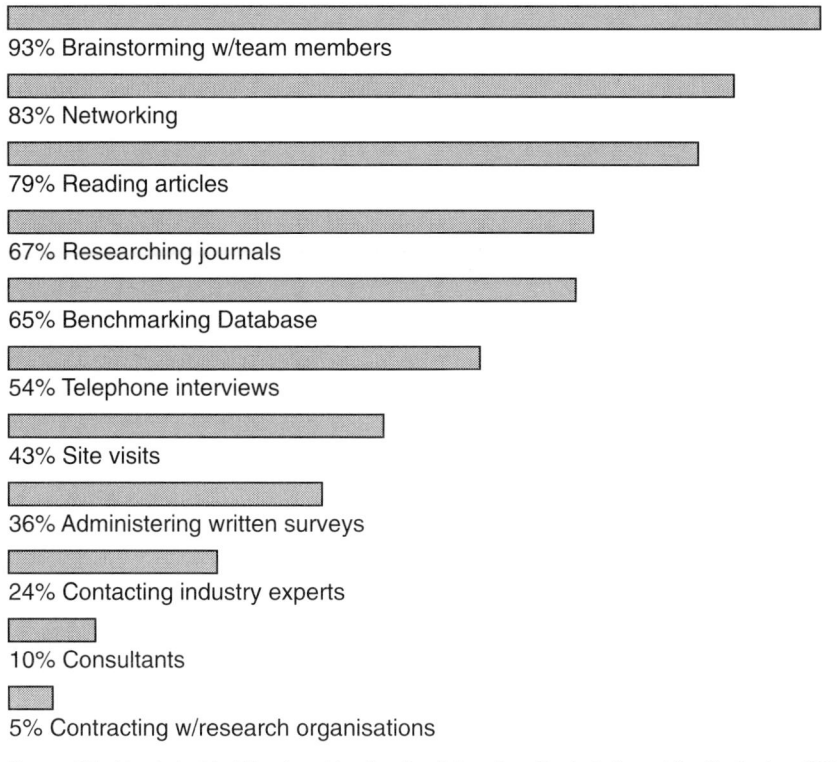

93% Brainstorming w/team members

83% Networking

79% Reading articles

67% Researching journals

65% Benchmarking Database

54% Telephone interviews

43% Site visits

36% Administering written surveys

24% Contacting industry experts

10% Consultants

5% Contracting w/research organisations

Source: 'Studying Industries' Benchmarking Practices', American Productivity and Quality Centre, 1992.

Figure 7.4   Data-gathering methods (N = 43)

Clearing House survey from 4 to 33.

DOCUMENTATION, DISSEMINATON AND IMPLEMENTATION OF STUDY RESULTS

Documentation methods vary greatly between companies in relation to Benchmarking and, as yet, no standardised format has emerged. Trip reports, presentations, statistical analyses and written reports are common, but vary greatly both within and between organisations. Many companies have developed their own pro formas for Benchmarking activities, but as yet these are not standardised.

The extent of internal dissemination of results within the company also varies. Seventy-six per cent of the American survey reported that Benchmarking study results are shared through presentation to top management and an overlapping 73 per cent disseminate study results through presentations to process owners. In addition, 64 per cent reported that the results were shared with teams and about 40 per cent that they convey the information through either company or Benchmarking newsletters. Organisations new to Benchmarking are often not very good at disseminating results and 16 per cent of the American survey indicated that study findings are only available upon request.

One of the most frustrating aspects of Benchmarking can be that having conducted a Benchmarking study and disseminated the information within the organisation, then nothing happens. Experience suggests that in most organisations foresight is required to ensure that Benchmarking study results do not just end up on somebody's shelf. Management must be aware from the beginning that, once they instigate Benchmarking activity, they cannot fail consistently to implement the superior practices that the studies reveal. None the less, internal marketing is necessary to ensure that the case for action is adequately made. In the American survey, the 2 factors which were identified as most influencing the actuality of implementation of results were whether management 'buy-in' to the findings and the return on investment (both 43 per cent). Process owner involvement and support was identified by 36 per cent of the respondents, cost of implementation by 20 per cent and the size of the performance gap by 14 per cent.

Benchmarking, like Quality Improvement, is by its nature a never-ending process. While it is often hard for the new starter to appreciate, the results of Benchmarking studies quickly become out of date and re-evaluation is continually required. In the American study, 32 per cent reported that they continually re-evaluate Benchmarking results, 9 per cent that this is done within 6 months, 17 per cent that this is done within 1 year and 30 per cent within 2 years. Interestingly, 12 per cent reported that they never re-evaluated the Benchmarking results – a very undesirable situation. In terms of re-Benchmarking a given process or competitor, a total of 45 per cent do this within 2 years and 85 per cent within 5 years. One cannot give general guidance on what the desirable time period is, since this will depend on factors such as competitive pressure, technology advancement and the company's commitment to Benchmarking and to 'being the best'. Clearly, however, Benchmarking should be seen as a continually re-evaluated activity.

MAKING IT WORK

For Benchmarking to be successful it is important for the practitioner to be aware of the requirements for success and the likely barriers. The accompanying strengths which support successful Benchmarking implementation are the obvious ones in terms of management support and commitment, leadership, a TQM programme or commitment to Quality, desire to change and improve, an economic imperative, and the existence of training and teamwork.

On the other hand, the obvious factors also get in the way. Lack of resources or the cost of the Benchmarking activity may be a problem. Lack of management commitment and support, inadequate training and skills, lack of understanding and awareness, poor planning and implementation, resistance to change and 'old thinking', the 'not invented here' mentality and the desire for 'quick fix' or short-term expectations only.

Those who do take the step, however, and keep at it, do view it as successful. In the American survey 48 per cent of the total sample believe that Benchmarking had already improved their products and services, while this rose to 72 per cent for those companies who had been conducting Benchmarking studies for 2 or more years. Clearly, it takes time and commitment to get the results from Benchmarking, and fighting the short-term thinking is what it is all about.

8 BENCHMARKING IN THE PUBLIC SECTOR

INTRODUCTION – THE PUBLIC SECTOR IS DIFFERENT

While Total Quality Management (TQM) and Benchmarking are as applicable to Public Administration as to private sector manufacturing and service industry, their application in Public Administration is more problematical. There are many reasons for this, including:

- Staff culture and the lack of individual ownership, responsibility, client-care and staff empowerment;
- Bureaucratic and non-responsive systems;
- Lack of clarity about the multiple customers and stakeholders involved in even single transactions;
- Political, as opposed to market-determined, levels and extent of service, especially for subsidised and zero-priced services;
- Problems of scale and complexity associated with the large, centralised organisations, sometimes with a large-scale technological basis.

The Public Administration sector, does, however, have a large potential for the development and improvement of its processes and procedures. This chapter explores the implementation of TQM and Best Practices Benchmarking within the public sector.

TQM ORIGINATES IN PUBLIC ADMINISTRATION

In many senses Public Administration is the most natural place for the introduction of a Total Quality Programme and Benchmarking. Bureaucratic administrative structures are more likely to exist here rather than in the commercial world, where financial and competitive pressures mitigates against the growth of bureaucracy and assist us in recalling quite clearly the purposes for the existence of the unit and the importance of the customer. Historically in Public Administration such clarity of purpose has not always been apparent and the importance of the 'customer need' has not always been paramount.

In Public Administration it has often been the case that the provision of the service to the public has not been that of a supplier to a customer, but rather that of an authority to a subject. Public Administration may not be deliberately belligerent or malevolent but none the less the Civil Servants within the Ministry concerned find themselves primarily as agents of the State carrying out an official State purpose, rather than service personnel involved in the provision of a defined service to a customer. Public Administration was after all a monopoly; there was little concept of realistic pricing of service against market alternatives and the punitive power was in the hands of the Public Administrator rather than the customer; it was not that the customer could withdraw their custom, but the Public Administrator could refuse to facilitate it.

Against this background, the need for the TQM revolution was clearly greater than in the private sector. It is no surprise, therefore, that apparently the first usage of the phrase 'Total Quality Management' was in the context of the American Department of Defense programme based upon the development of ideas of Deming and many others.

The further development of TQM has not neglected the areas of Public Administration or Public Service. In the UK, US and the world, Government Departments, Government Agencies, Public Utilities and uniformed and non-uniformed public services have been amongst the forefront in TQM. This very much reflects the development of ideas such as the Citizens' Charter and general pressure from various sources such as the Cabinet Office.

Indeed, Professor Tony Bendell's (East Midlands Electricity Professor of Quality Management at the Nottingham Trent University) special relationship with East Midland Electricity is typical of the importance of TQM and Quality Assurance in the transfer of public service organisations from Public Administration to private sector public utilities. This interest can currently be seen across UK public utilities and in the preparation for the pursuit of Agency status by Branches within British Government Public Administration. Active interest can be seen, too, in Government Departments; from the Department of Employment, to the Ministry of Defence, from the Inland Revenue to the Defence Research Agency, from the Health Service to the police force, from the fire service to education and training, from forensic science to British Railways.

THE APPLICATION OF TQM IN PUBLIC ADMINISTRATION

While the need is great and the origins early, the application of TQM and Benchmarking in Public Administration are particularly difficult. There are many reasons for this and one of the foremost is cultural. While, increasingly, Public Administration is needing to move closer to the 'real world' in terms of financial accountability, management, Quality Assurance, and productivity and effectiveness, none the less, the history of Public Administration is one in which staff could be expected to have a job for life, to rise on time – served or perhaps connections, to have little incentive and much disincentive to show ingenuity, new thinking or effective teamwork and, above all, not to question the system.

This backdrop is one to which concepts of TQM and Benchmarking will seem particularly alien and this can make the process of getting TQM established very difficult. Thus staff culture, the lack of individual ownership of the work, of the process of the Public Administration function, or of the customer relationship, together with lack of responsibility and any concept of client-care or staff-empowerment all represent negatives that need to be overcome by the design and implementation of the TQM programme.

The systems themselves, in Public Administration, also often tend to be bureaucratic and non-responsive. The lack of the incentive of the market place for quick response, flexibility, simplicity and the availability of information on short timescales means that introducing these requirements as needs within a TQM programme, is once again a big step. Bureaucracy and non-responsive systems are not just in themselves the opposite of what we are trying to achieve within TQM, they also hinder its introduction and development and slow its progress.

Even where there is the will to transform Public Administration towards a TQM culture, systems and management style, technical problems still remain due to the limited nature of the TQM models currently in general use. A major orientation of most TQM models is the predominance of the *customer* in the purpose of the organisation and its infrastructure. In Public Administration, this single-customer focus is not so clear; it is not just that there are multiple types of customers, but rather that there are multiple customers and stakeholders involved in even single transactions. For example, when a police officer arrests a potential criminal, is the officer's customer the criminal, the victim, witnesses, the courts, the Home Office or the community?

Public service organisations have attempted to solve this technical difficulty with the concepts of TQM by the introduction of the *stakeholder* concept. Stakeholder models can now be found in many aspects of Public Administration and Public Service worldwide. For example, the Royal Mail identify their stakeholders as customers, employees, shareholders and the community, while East Midlands Electricity adds suppliers.

The problem, however, is that these generic stakeholder groups can tend to be somewhat unfocused in themselves. The community is, by its nature, a very large and in-homogeneous group with divergent opinions on divergent issues. Lack of focus is what we are trying to avoid with TQM and Benchmarking, and so much has to be done in the attempt to clarify. Even where this is done, down at the operational level in the process of Public Administration there is still a problem. Staff have to have clear priorities in their relations to the various stakeholder groups so that the organisation can be focused towards their purpose for existing. This requires clear policy from the top, as well as staff discussion at all levels.

Another problem is that in Public Administration the market itself does not determine the level and extent of service. Decisions are taken at a political level and broadly there may be no limit to the demand for a zero priced or subsidised service. This then creates shortfalls in the availability in service provision which appear to the consumer/customer as inefficiencies. The consequence is that confusion can remain in the customer's mind, the public, between productivity and Quality. This problem is inbuilt into the nature of Public Administration and represents a particular challenge for the staff involved.

Yet another problem is that Public Administration may necessitate large, centralised organisations, with associated complexity and problems of scale, combined with a bureaucratic management style. This implies that most employees will be a 'long way from the customer'. Even front-line employees suffer, since they are a long way from decision making and are themselves at the mercy of the internal systems. Such problems may be exacerbated if the organisation has a large-scale technological basis, such as in nationalised power provision, or a dependence upon a major computer system, such as perhaps in tax collection.

STRATEGIES FOR SUCCESS IN THE PUBLIC SECTOR

As indicated previously, the potential problems of implementation of a TQM programme and Benchmarking within the organisational structure of Public Administration are many. Consequently, it is essential that strategies for success are sought both in relation to the implementation of TQM as well as in the implementation of Benchmarking best practice. The following examines some of those strategies for success, as well as looking at how the public sector as a whole has responded to this challenge. It also looks briefly at the situation in the US, where TQM has been successfully implemented into Federal Departments.

TQM should become part of the 'real work' of a Public Sector Department or Unit as early as possible. Senior management must realise that TQM cannot be delegated and that it is sensible for a Steering Group of the most senior managers to be set up at Departmental/Agency level to facilitate the transformation in the organisation. Ideally, this should be chaired by the most senior officer. For it is only in this way that TQM can become part of the overall job. The Steering Group will be able to identify and focus on the mission of the organisation, the stakeholder groups, the intrinsic values and their purpose for existing. The whole of the workforce should be involved in the Quality improvement process, but it should commence top-down before returning bottom-up. While employee training will be necessary, two important aspects should be taken into consideration.

First, middle managers should be adequately prepared for the change in behaviours and, indeed, of attitude which will be expected and required of them for the programme to be successful. Second, cascade training is preferable to 'wall-to-wall' indoctrination.

In cascade training, the members of the Steering Group themselves explain to their own direct reports what the TQM programme is about, what they are intending to do in their own area, and perhaps come up with suggestions as to what their direct reports may wish to do and ask what do they think. At each level down the hierarchy, the same process is repeated; each manager explaining to his or her own direct reports what it is all about and discussing how it may be implemented within their employee's area and what might be tackled first. With this system, each employee can put TQM in the context of their own job, which is typically not the reality with wall-to-wall training. It also dramatically reduces the amount of help that the Public Administrator will need from outside consultants, although it is conventional for consultants to assist in the preparation of materials for cascade training and in the nature of the pro-gramme. Such assistance by experienced consultants is extremely important; and to this end the consultant may tem-porarily join the Quality Steering Group.

A systematic approach to the quantification of quality and improvement within Public Administration is also highly desirable, since otherwise the programme can be unfocused. This may be initially undertaken by a Cost of Quality approach or subsequently by the development of Critical Success Factors. Both systems represent a unified approach to measurement, whether by looking at all the money that is wasted by doing things wrong and the prevention costs involved or, in the case of Critical Success Factors, by identifying the small group of (preferably less than eight) Critical Success Factors on which the progress of the organisation will be judged. These measures then provide a yardstick for improvement activities lower down in the organisation. Priority activities are those which impact on the measures most heavily.

TQM AND BENCHMARKING IN US PUBLIC ADMINISTRATION

Evidence of the growth of TQM in the public sector is illustrated by the situation in the US where, over the 1980s, TQM has become a prominent feature of Public Administration. Both NASA and the Department of Defense, during the Reagan and Bush administrations, made sustained efforts in relation to the implementation of TQM, as did other Federal Departments and Agencies. Indeed, TQM has been implemented in 19 of the largest Federal Departments and agencies.

It is the Federal Quality Institute (FQI), which has largely been instrumental in the promotion of TQM in Public Administration within the US Government. The FQI, established in 1988, is part of the Executive Office of the President and acts as a primary source of leadership, information and consultancy service on quality management in the Federal Government. In the FQI handbook, seven criteria are identified which are seen as determining the success of quality efforts within federal departments. These are:

- Top management support;
- Customer focus;
- Long-term strategic planning;
- Employee training and recognition;
- Employee empowerment and teamwork;
- Measurement;
- Quality Assurance.

Moreover, the above criteria reflect the scoring guidelines used to judge Federal organisations applying for the President's Award for Quality and Productivity Improvement. Winners of the award, and the award criteria themselves, can be used as Benchmarks to which public sector organisations can compare their performance. The award was established in 1989 and its award criteria reflect the criteria for the American Malcolm

Baldrige National Quality Award as well as the Japanese Deming Prize.

Alongside this award, the FQI administers a scheme of Quality Improvement Prototype Awards or QIPs. These are given annually to Federal Departments as a recognition of excellence in implementing TQM and achieving quality improvement results. The winner then acts as a model or Benchmark for the rest of the Government Service; they prepare videotapes and case studies, and present workshops about their organisations.

Over the period 1988–91 there have been 15 QIP winners, ranging from branches of the Inland Revenue Service to the Naval Publications and Forms Center, with reported savings of between $10 million and $704 million in one year. In each year, there are three or four finalists for every winner.

QUALITY OF SERVICE AND BENCHMARKING IN THE UK PUBLIC SECTOR

In November 1991 a consortium was formed and sponsored by the Development Division of the Cabinet Office, which is now subsumed into the Office of Public Service and Science (OPSS). This consisted of 12 project leaders from 11 different departments and agencies. Their primary objective was to:

> encourage, co-ordinate and support projects . . . which will enable departments and agencies to achieve demonstrable and continuous improvements in the quality of service they provide.

Their aim was one of improving the quality of service offered by departments and agencies by taking into account best practice from both the public and private sector. The 11 different departments and agencies which were involved in the project were as follows:

- Benefits Agency (Central Derbyshire District);
- Central Office of Information;
- Civil Service College (London Centre);
- Employment Service;
- Health and Safety Executive (Research and Laboratory Services Divisions);
- Home Office (Immigration Service);
- Inland Revenue (Capital Taxes Office and the Accounts Office, Cumbernauld);
- Lord Chancellors' Department (South-Eastern Circuit);
- Patent Office;
- Public Record Office;
- Department of Trade and Industry (North East).

The main focus of the programme was the development of standards relating to quality of service. This was achieved by the establishment of measures of quality of service which then enabled the setting of realistic standards derived from the priorities set down by their customers. Research, therefore, had to be carried out in order to establish exactly what constituted the priorities of customers. Current performance could then be established, as well as targets for improvement of the service provided. Members of the consortium developed a twofold approach to this situation; first they established measures which related to customers' understanding of the service and their degree of satisfaction with it, as well as establishing measures which related to the effective delivery of the service, from this they were able to use this information to set standards or Benchmarks for future provision of the service.

The first stage was to gather initial data which then acted as a base for the establishment of measurement and performance Benchmarks which then enabled the members of the consortium to identify key issues to measure. Research methods were used for the establishment of satisfaction measures, the establishment of performance Benchmarks and standards to review the effect and impact of changes in service methods (e.g. new services, different facilities), and to provide information to enable improvement and innovations to be implemented. Four areas were taken into consideration when measuring the quality of service, convenience of service, facilities and amenities available, provision of information, personal treatment.

Measurement against a set of standards is essential to the achievement of superior performance in any organisation, whether in the public or private sector. There were three categories of measurement that the consortium took into consideration when setting targets to be achieved. These consisted of product, process and customer satisfaction.

Product measures were defined as those measures which focus on the fundamental issues which an organisation believes are important to its customers. They are used to measure the satisfaction of the customer in relation to the processes of the service given to the customer. Satisfaction measures were defined as relating directly to the customer's interaction with the actual organisation itself, while process measures were defined as relating to the running of the organisation, those internal processes relating to the operational efficiency of the service.

From this information specific targets could then be set in different departments. For example, in relation to response times, the Patent Office set a target of trying to reply in detail to correspondence within four to six weeks, as well as issuing examination reports within three months. At the Accounts Office (Cumbernauld) a target was set of processing 100 per cent of Giro credits by the day following receipt. And in the Capital Taxes Office they set themselves a target for 80 per cent of correspondence to be dealt with within 28 days and 95 per cent within 56 days.

It is also interesting to note some of the standards which the consortium decided to Benchmark performance against. The appearance of the Citizens' Charter has provided an added incentive for the improvement in the quality of service. The Charter itself lays down distinctive aims in relation to the standards to measure performance against. The aims of the Charter are to work for better quality in every public service, to give people more choice, to make sure that everyone is told what kind of service they can reasonably expect to receive and to make sure that people know what to do if something goes wrong.

The Charter Standard established six key principles for the level of performance which can reasonably be expected from the public sector. These are as follows:

1 Publication of the standards of service that the customer can reasonably expect and of performance against those standards;
2 Evidence that the view of those who use the service have been taken into account in setting standards;
3 Clear information about the range of services provided, in plain language;
4 Courteous and efficient customer service, from staff who are normally prepared to identify themselves by name;
5 Well-signposted avenues for complaint if the customer is not satisfied, with some means of independent review wherever possible; and
6 Independent evaluation of performance against standards and a clear commitment to providing value for money.

The Charter Mark scheme was established to recognise achievement against these standards with up to 50 Charter Marks being awarded annually. In the case study, all members of that project sought to apply the Charter Standards in their work with several of them applying for Charter Marks.

Other sources which provided a standard to Benchmark against were the criteria of the Malcolm Baldrige National Quality Award (US) and the European Quality Award. These were found to provide valuable sources for quality improvement, as well as representing standards against which to Benchmark their own performance.

9 BENCHMARKING IN OTHER DIFFICULT AREAS – R & D, DESIGN AND THE CREATIVE SERVICE SECTOR

INTRODUCTION – DEALING WITH CREATIVITY

In many senses creative people, or creative activities or departments are the most difficult when attempting to introduce quality improvement and Total Quality Management (TQM). There is a natural aversion to quality assurance among the creative, since they believe it will stifle creativity and cannot be applied in an area which is 'not like making soap powder'. In many senses this is as true among engineers and scientists in Research and Development (R & D) as it is among graphic designers, interior designers, journalists, chefs, textile designers and performing artists.

This apparent inbuilt conflict between the free thought of creativity and the restrictions of structure associated with quality systems is not new and it remains one of the major challenges for the spread of implementation of ISO 9000 within the service sector. Such systems, however, do not have to be stifling of creativity and this justification or objection in any case masks other background concerns – fear of change and increased monitoring, lack of clarity of purpose, inability to find suitable measures of productivity and performance, and the like. With the correct level of senior management commitment and appropriate education, it is not fundamentally difficult to overcome these objections, although without this, these objections can be major delaying factors.

For TQM, rather than quality assurance, there is even less excuse that it stifles creativity, since the very purpose of TQM is to build the self-improving organisation, putting to work the creativity of every individual within the organisation, not just within their core jobs of work, but in order to improve the organisation itself. Nevertheless, a common objection to TQM among creative professionals is that it is not appropriate to them and that, reading between the lines, it belongs in a manufacturing plant.

Clearly, progress is now being made in the introduction of Total Quality concepts into the broad spectrum of R & D, design and the creative service sector. The introduction of Benchmarking into these areas as part of, or apart from, the introduction of TQM is particularly problematical. These areas are historically poorly systematised, so that defining business processes, finding Benchmarking grids and finding meaningful comparisons, externally or even internally, are extremely difficult. Fortuitously, this problem is increasingly recognised and attention is increasingly being focused on how to approach it.

Following the introduction of Japanese approaches into management and production, R&D and product development is now under attack from Japanese Simultaneous Engineering practices. Justification for the introduction of these approaches, like those that have gone before in manufacturing and management, is based on a broad, crude Benchmark of Western performance in these areas with that of Japanese companies. The whole area represents a Benchmark of traditional Western development processes against Japanese ones in order primarily to accelerate time to market, cut development costs and failures.

SIMULTANEOUS ENGINEERING

The need for Simultaneous Engineering can be seen by looking at some of the things that are currently wrong in our design and development processes. The sorts of quotes that we often get that processes 'do not work', that the handover to manufacturing has 'taken place too early', that the area is 'not making soap powder' and that 'you cannot timetable creativity', illustrates the difficulty of applying quality tools and approaches to this area. Typically, in the design and development process we see backtracking and cycling, we see escalating costs, late delivery, poor quality and very often products which eventually are hard to make. There are also questions like: 'Does the customer really want what it is that we have designed?' And there are inter-departmental fences and suspicions, and fights and blame. There are barriers to information flow and we see our technical prima donnas, experts, and the isolation aspects and lack of teamwork.

Perhaps most notable of all, there is a lack of focusing tools such as Quality Function Deployment, Failure Modes and Effects Analysis, and Taguchi methods. There is also a lack of a comprehensive approach, a lack of discipline, a lack of clarity of purpose, and a lack of early involvement of suppliers and departments. The phrase often used to describe our current approach to development and design is 'over the fence engineering', whereby we eventually throw the product design over the fence, and manufacturing has to pick it up and do something with it. This, of course, causes panic and disruption, and indeed dubious quality.

Just as TQM has had its various pseudonyms, so does Simultaneous Engineering, often being described as Parallel Engineering or Concurrent Engineering. In any case, the name is not so important. What we need to do, as with TQM, is to purpose-build for your company and, whether you call it Simultaneous Engineering in your design area, or Quality Improvement, it all comes to the same thing. The basic keys in TQM in the design and development process are the need for multi-disciplinary task forces, the need to define the product in customer terms and translate them into engineering terms, the need to optimise products and processes, and the need to design for manufacturing assembly. The special feature of Simultaneous Engineering is the simultaneous development of product, manufacturing equipment and processes, as well as quality control and marketing.

The methods of Simultaneous Engineering developed in Japan in the 1970s and 1980s, with names associated with the approach being those of Honda, Mazda, Nissan and Panasonic. In the US it was not until the mid-1980s that we began to see the applications of Simultaneous Engineering in Chrysler, Ford, General Motors, Xerox and Digital. European applications have also been largely associated with the automotive industry such as Volkswagen, Daimler-Benz, Opel, Fiat and also Krupp.

One feature of the approach of Simultaneous Engineering is the application of interfunctional task teams in much the same way that TQM uses these in other aspects of the business. In these teams we see representatives from product design engineering, from manufacturing engineering, from marketing, from purchasing, from finance, from suppliers and from customers. Various team options are sometimes applied; the most successful approach perhaps being to have a simple pre-concept team of four or five individuals which is eventually expanded to a full task force at the concept stage. One reason for the success of Simultaneous Engineering in Japanese companies is that large Japanese manufacturers tend to make their own special purpose machines or at least make them through subsidiaries. This is the pattern, for instance, in Honda, Nissan, Toyota and Mazda. This makes it easier to involve manufacturing engineers at an early stage.

A potential conflict between the approach of Simultaneous

Engineering and the wider approach of TQM is the treatment of data. Simultaneous Engineering tends to aim for data integration. One quote is that Simultaneous Engineering is 'wasted without CAD-CAM' and there is a desire to integrate data throughout the organisation, right through from design to manufacture. In TQM we have tended to concentrate on the use of process data rather than historic data and, if we follow the approaches associated with Ishikawa, we tend to collect data as necessary and not set up large databases.

It is of interest to compare the bar charts for our conventional approach to engineering with those for Simultaneous Engineering as in Figure 9.1. In the conventional approach to engineering, we tend to start each stage of design and development later than in the Simultaneous Engineering approach. This gives us much greater time using Simultaneous Engineering to bring the product to the market in a safe and acceptable form.

Indeed, if we compare the Japanese and American automotive industries, we see that not only are there more engineering changes in the American automotive industry, but also, unfortunately, that these tend to take place at a later stage than in the Japanese industry: Figure 9.2. The consequence of this is that we are often problem solving after we have moved into the production phase. This, of course, is the worst time to problem solve, as early changes are much easier and cheaper to accomplish than subsequent ones. It also illustrates the point that Japanese companies can typically develop products much more quickly than their European contemporaries.

A consequence of late changes in the design and development process is that we tend to overshoot on timescales. This has a serious implication in terms of costing. It means that we are in negative revenue for considerably longer and that, when we do eventually break through into positive revenue, we have lost the potential for much of the gain we may have made because we are not perhaps first into the market.

	Activity		Concept development	Design development	Design validation	Production development
CONVENTIONAL ENGINEERING	Marketing and Product Planning		▓			
	Engineering		▓▓▓			
	Testing			▓▓▓		
	Manufacturing				▓▓▓	
SIMULTANEOUS ENGINEERING	Marketing and Product Planning		▓▓			
	Engineering	Feasibility	▓			
		Production design	▓▓			
	Testing	New technology	▓▓			
		Main programme		▓▓▓		
	Manufacturing	Feasibility/ tolerancing	▓▓▓			
		Tool studies	▓▓			
		Tooling			▓▓▓	

Figure 9.1

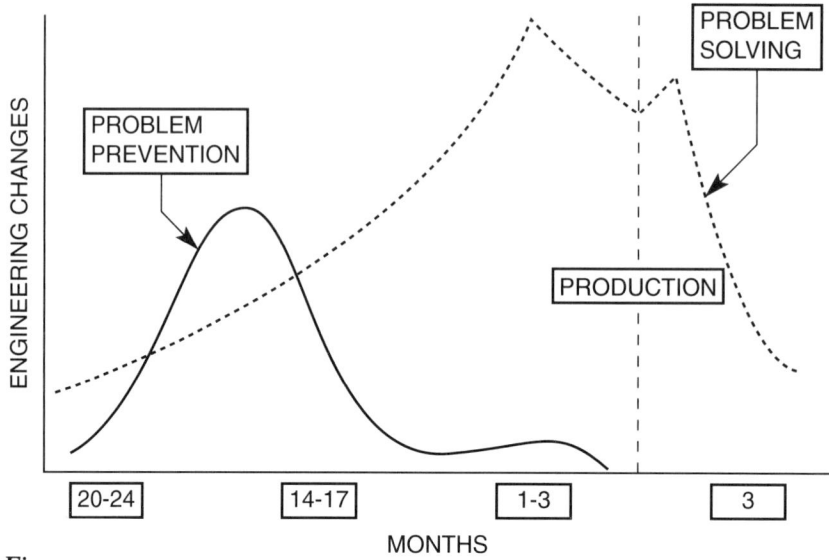

Figure 9.2

QUALITY FUNCTION DEPLOYMENT

The two major tools of Simultaneous Engineering are Quality Function Deployment (QFD) and Taguchi methodology. QFD is a team-based methodology for incorporating the Voice of the Customer in the design, development, manufacturing and marketing activities of the organisation. Taguchi methodology, in contrast, is an experimentally-based prototyping approach, which can be employed at the various stages in the development of product or service.

An interesting aspect of QFD is that it incorporates a Benchmarking activity as part of the incorporation of the Voice of the Customer into product or service design, development, manufacturing and marketing.

QFD originates from Mitsubishi Heavy Industries in the early 1970s and was taken up by Toyota Autobody in the late 1970s. QFD is best thought of as an approach rather than a technique, since, like other Japanese methodologies it relies heavily on teamwork, and much of the benefit comes out of clear, concise team planning and communication.

QFD is a planning technique to ensure that the design of both products and processes are customer focused. It uses a series of matrices – Houses of Quality – to link customer needs with product or process features. On each matrix, customer needs are represented by rows, and product or process features or 'hows' are represented by columns. The body of the matrix gives the strength of relationships between needs and the way they will be, or are being, met. The roof of the house gives the correlation between the hows and the right-hand wing of the house gives a Benchmark of performance in satisfying the needs against major competitors or possibly best practice. These aspects of the Houses of Quality tend to be fairly standard, but other aspects tend to vary between applications. A basic House of Quality is illustrated in Figure 9.3. The bullseye symbol is used to represent a strong relationship, a circle a medium relationship and a triangle a weak relationship. Sometimes

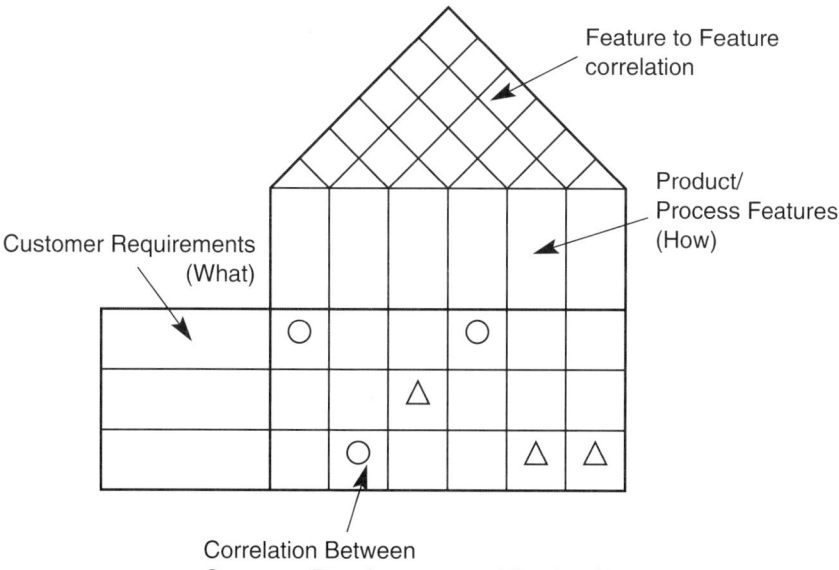

Figure 9.3   Quality Function Deployment – House of Quality

these are reserved for positive relationships only, with different symbols for the equivalent negative ones.

A further example is shown in Figure 9.4. This represents a House of Quality for a retail laundry. From the House we see that a survey of customers has revealed that what matters to the customers are that the clothes are Completely Clean, that there is Perfect Press, that the Correct Clothes are returned and the Correct Service provided, and that there is a Quick Turn Around and a Friendly Service. The customer survey also revealed that what was of most importance to the customer was not that the clothes were completely clean, but instead that the correct clothes were returned and the correct service was given. Accordingly, in the table this is represented by a weighting of five. The second most important aspect was viewed by the customer as a Friendly Service (four), then Quick Turn Around (three), then Perfect Press (two), then Completely Clean (one).

The retail laundry sees its achievement of these five customer requirements to be obtained through the six operating requirements identified as columns of the House of Quality. These are Good Training, Correct Washing/Bleaching Formulation, Correct Wash Programme, Clean Tumbler Filters, Correct Moisture Prior to Calendering and Good Equipment Maintenance. Looking at the body of the table, we see that the most important aspect to the customer, Correct Clothes and Correct Service, only has a single (medium) relationship to one of the operating requirements – Good Training. This is also true for the second most important aspect to the customer – Friendly Service. The next most important aspect to the customer – a Quick Turnaround – also has a weak dependence on Good Equipment Maintenance. Interestingly enough, it is only the two least important customer requirements out of the five that we have identified, which are well supported by the operating requirements inside the organisation; Perfect Press has a strong relationship with Correct

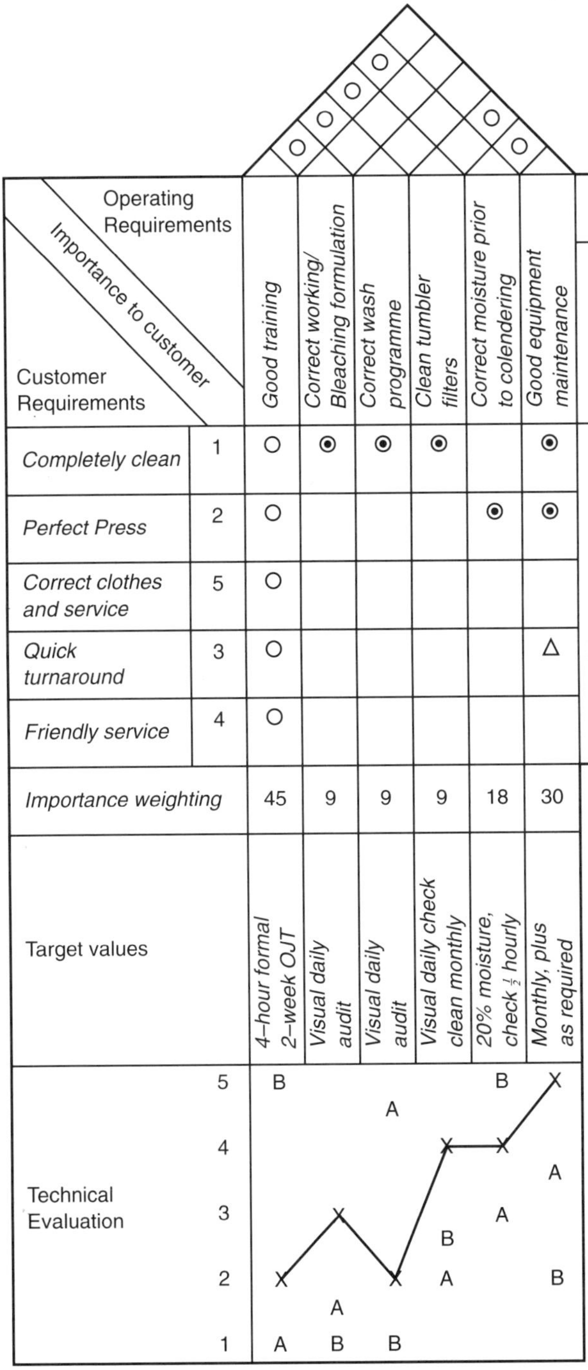

Figure 9.4   Quality Function Deployment in a retail laundry

Moisture Prior to Calendering and Good Equipment Maintenance, as well as its medium relationship with Good Training. Completely Clean Clothes depends strongly on the Correct Washing/Bleaching Formulation, the Correct Wash Programme, the Cleanness of the Tumbler Filters and Good Equipment Maintenance as well as having a medium relationship with Good Training.

In the roof of the House of Quality we see the relationships between the various operating requirements that satisfy the customer requirements. Good Training has medium relationships with the provision of the Correct Wash/Bleach Formulation, the provision of the Correct Wash Programme, the provision of Clean Tumbler Filters and the provision of Correct Moisture Prior to Calendering. Good Equipment Maintenance has medium relationships with Clean Tumbler Filters and Correct Moisture Prior to Calendering. Other relationships, of course, may exist in reality.

The importance of the various operating requirements may be calculated from the importance of the customer requirements and the weightings given by the correlations in the body of the table. As an illustration, consider Friendly Service – this has a customer importance weighting of four and is connected to Good Training by a medium relationship which has a weighting of three. Friendly Service, then, contributes 4 times 3, which equals 12, to the importance weighting of Good Training. Proceeding in a similar way with each of the other four customer requirements, and in each case multiplying by three (because of the medium relationships with Good Training) and then adding up each of the contributions, we come to a total importance weighting of 45 for Good Training. For each of the other measures, proceeding similarly, we obtain the importance weightings shown in the table.

From these weightings it is clear that Good Training is the most important operating requirement, not because any customer requirement depends strongly on it, but because all customer requirements are related to it, albeit only by medium relationships. The next most important operating requirement is Good Equipment Maintenance, followed some way back by Correct Moisture Prior to Calendering. The three remaining operating requirements are of equal importance. These weightings will help to prioritise effort in terms of meeting the customer requirement. Clearly here, most effort must be given to ensuring and maintaining Good Training and Good Equipment Maintenance.

If we now consider the right-hand wing of the House of Quality, this contains information which Benchmarks our performance as a retail laundry against that of our main competitors. For example, for Completely Clean Clothes we can see that our customers have given us a rating of four, on a five-point scale on which five is the best, against a rating of three-and-a-half for our competitor B, and of two for our competitor A. We are clearly doing better. This is also true in terms of Perfect Press, where we are well ahead of both our competitors. We are also ahead on Friendly Service. However, we are behind on Correct Clothes and Service, and Quick Turnaround. This is particularly important for Correct Clothes and Service, because this is regarded as most important by our customers. This Benchmarking enables us to see that we must improve on Correct Clothes and Service, and Quick Turnaround to have a competitive edge over our competitors.

The basement of the House of Quality contains the calculated importance weightings, and also target values and technical evaluations. The target values represent the targets on the operating requirements. The technical evaluation represents Benchmarking our operating requirements against those of our competitors.

In product development applications of Quality Function Deployment, a single House of Quality would not be used, but several, as is illustrated in Figure 9.5. The first house (Product Planning) would translate customer wants into design

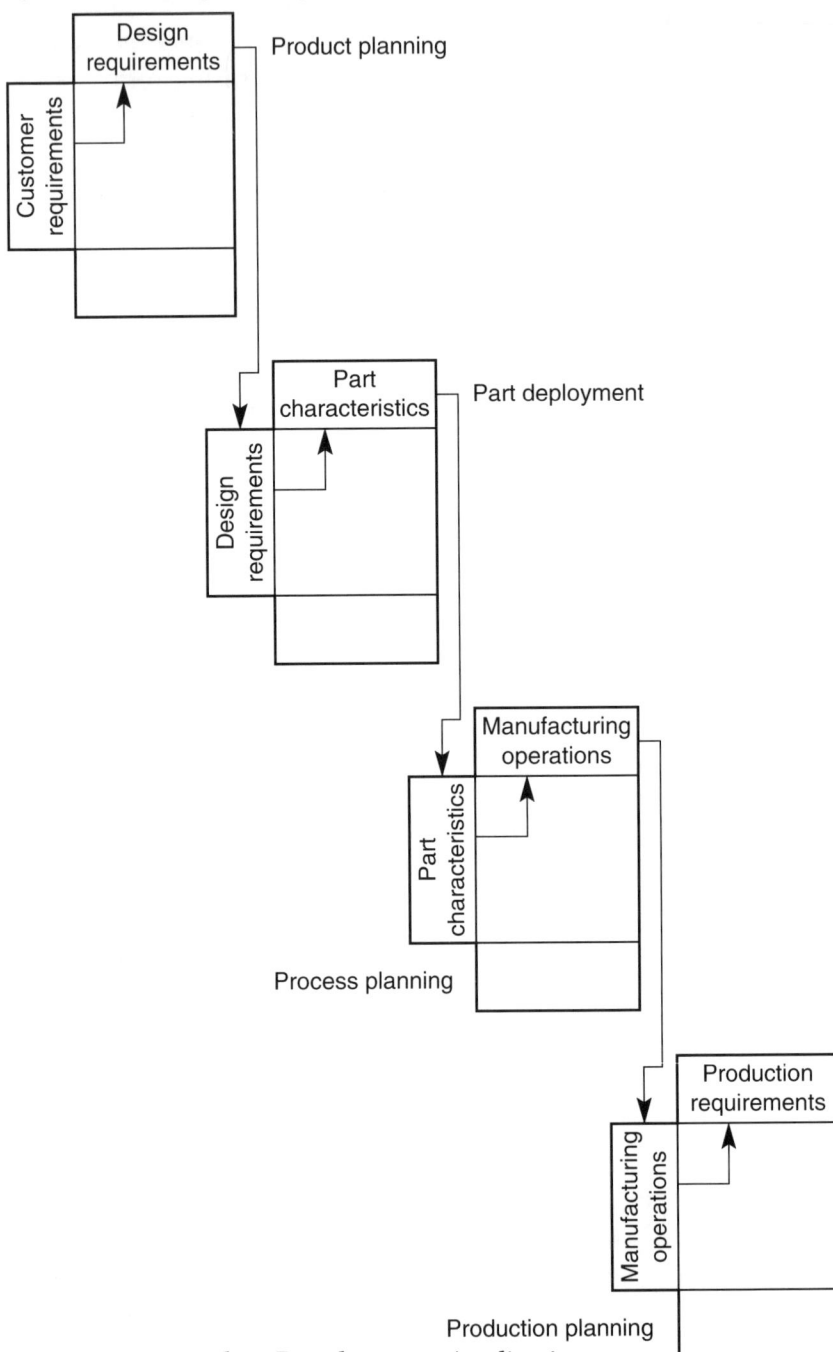

*Figure 9.5   Product Development Application
of Quality Function Deployment*

requirements. These then form the input to the second house (Part Deployment) where design requirements are mapped to part characteristics. In the third house (Process Planning) part characteristics are mapped to key process operations, and in the fourth house (Production Planning) key process operations are mapped to production requirements. Other houses may be introduced as needed, for example for installation, if appropriate.

Applied correctly, Quality Function Deployment should make use of an interfunctional team composed of representatives of all those involved in, or with interests in, the development of the product, or service, from market research through design, development, manufacturing and delivery to the customer. Small teams are preferable, of six to eight individuals of equal status. Specialists may be co-opted as needed. Open minds are needed, as well as experience.

Attendance at the series of team meetings should be a high priority. On major projects, perhaps as many as 60 hours or more of meetings may be required. These need to be in the project plan. Teams need training, and consensus, rather than voting, should be the order of operation among the personnel from production planning, research, design and development, marketing, product engineering, manufacturing, purchasing, service, installation, quality and tooling who may be involved.

First projects need careful implementation. Teams should be chosen carefully, as should be the project, and both should be monitored to ensure that things do not go wrong.

One possible set of steps for applying Quality Function Deployment (in development) is shown in Figure 9.6. It is apparent that no high technology is needed to use this approach, although specialist software has been marketed in this area. Little training in the technique is required, although training and mentoring is necessary to change the work pattern, to establish discipline and to help to remove the functional barriers. Also, little specialist skill is required since the complexity, which might at first sight be apparent in the method, really arises because we are no longer overlooking data which are overlooked in the conventional approach. There is also no knowledge loss, or repetition of work, with the QFD approach, and accordingly time and resource reductions claimed can be in the range from a half to one-third. However, it must be stated that this is in companies who are mature in the use of QFD. First projects may add to normal development times. The use of QFD should include both basic and excitement features – in the case of the laundry, for instance, the basic cleaning process was not the most important aspect to the customer, who took this for granted. Similarly with an automobile, it is the aesthetic design features, not the basic functionality, which is often most attractive to a customer.

Used properly, QFD ensures discipline, structure and conformance to timescales which have been clearly stated. It also ensures a team attitude and breaches functional boundaries. It ensures recognition of customer satisfaction, and the anticipation and prioritisation of customer needs. As a consequence of its use the customer only gets, and only pays for, what they require, and it helps in the development of a whole life-cycle attitude. QFD presents a continuous thread of information and communication throughout the organisation. All aspects of quality of customer service are covered. It helps ensure attention to detail and detailed pre-planning. As a consequence of its use, actions and resources are also moved upstream, informed decisions are made and complex interactions clarified. By QFD we achieve problem avoidance which gives us competitive advantage. Some benefits of QFD are shown in Figure 9.7.

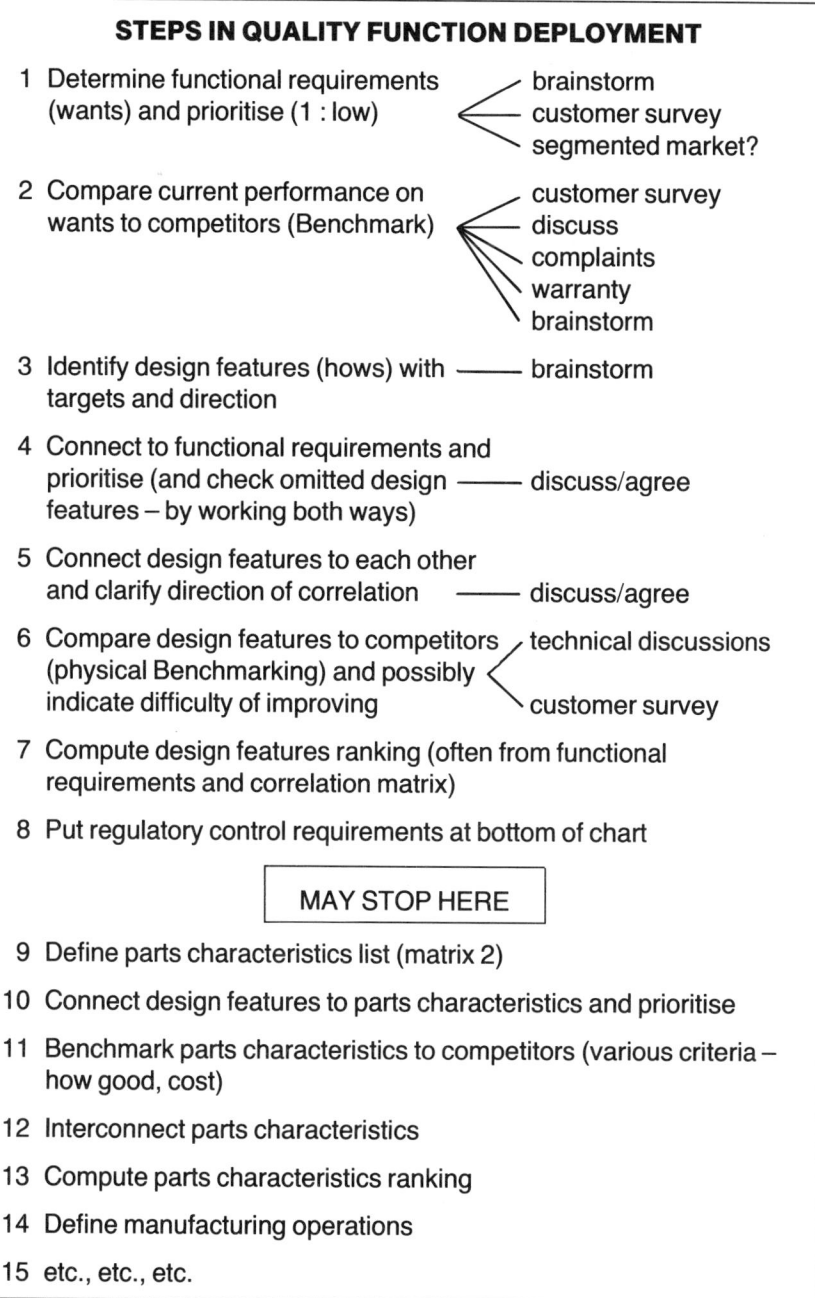

STEPS IN QUALITY FUNCTION DEPLOYMENT

1 Determine functional requirements (wants) and prioritise (1 : low) — brainstorm / customer survey / segmented market?

2 Compare current performance on wants to competitors (Benchmark) — customer survey / discuss / complaints / warranty / brainstorm

3 Identify design features (hows) with —— brainstorm targets and direction

4 Connect to functional requirements and prioritise (and check omitted design —— discuss/agree features – by working both ways)

5 Connect design features to each other and clarify direction of correlation —— discuss/agree

6 Compare design features to competitors — technical discussions (physical Benchmarking) and possibly indicate difficulty of improving — customer survey

7 Compute design features ranking (often from functional requirements and correlation matrix)

8 Put regulatory control requirements at bottom of chart

MAY STOP HERE

9 Define parts characteristics list (matrix 2)

10 Connect design features to parts characteristics and prioritise

11 Benchmark parts characteristics to competitors (various criteria – how good, cost)

12 Interconnect parts characteristics

13 Compute parts characteristics ranking

14 Define manufacturing operations

15 etc., etc., etc.

Figure 9.6   Steps in Quality Function Deployment

- Improved quality
- Improved product reliability
- Reduced warranty claims
- Lower cost in design and manufacture
- Opportunity for improved profitability and improved company performance
- Reduced decision/planning time and improved decision making
- Improved productivity of technical and other staff
- A more customer-orientated workforce
- Better reaction to marketing opportunities

Figure 9.7   Some benefits of Quality Function Deployment

To achieve these advantages and benefits, however, QFD must:

- be team-based;
- have coherence;
- have access to full market information;
- be documented at each stage;
- be reviewed and agreed at the next meeting;
- be based on individuals bringing information into the meetings and doing work between meetings;
- be team-based not committee-based;
- be disciplined;
- focus on voice of customer;
- have top-level commitment;
- be open to the customer; and
- be viewed as a process, not as a technique.

The difficulties that tend to arise in the applications of QFD are in themselves really advantages, since they force the clarification of issues which are often only implicit in the conventional approach. Thus, they force the resolution of these issues and the consistency of the development programme. Some such difficulties are shown in Figure 9.8.

1 Ignorant customers – especially on needs

2 Too late decisions or authorisation to proceed

3 Lack of clarity in responsibility/authorisation to define

4 Changes (iterations), e.g. in design features
   by others/management
   late
   in conflict with design philosophy or parts
   procurement policy etc.

5 Non-standard features/orders

6 Lack of attention to detail

7 First project and team

Figure 9.8   Difficulties over advantages in clarification

QFD has a good record of use in Japan, the US and, increasingly, Europe. Companies such as Rank Xerox, Ford and DEC have achieved, in some cases, staggering results from the use of QFD techniques. However, automotive applications are still probably among the most common.

QFD techniques are often introduced as part of Simultaneous Engineering or Concurrent Engineering. In the Simultanenous Engineering approach, a multidisciplinary task force is used as management, at a higher level, to ensure that there is simultaneous development of product, manufacturing equipment and processes, quality control and marketing. The product is defined in customer terms and translated into engineering terms by QFD.

Various versions of QFD and extensions to QFD have been developed. Numerous forms of Houses of Quality are in use within certain organisations, such as Motorola. A particularly interesting example of the extension of QFD, is that developed by Florida Power and Light (first international prize winners of the Deming Prize), known as the Table of Tables. This is a matrix that cross-relates customer requirements and specific quality elements in internal administration, but which also pulls together all the different major customer groups within a single table.

Florida Power and Light (FPL) see a number of steps in their process of generating a Table of Tables. First, they decide who the customers are; that is, they identify the major customer groups by deaggregating the total market and services provided. The second step is to survey the customers to obtain data on needs. These are then weighted for importance and grouped into 19 quality elements. These elements include courteous customer service, continuity of service, environmental protection and so on.

The fourth stage is to begin to determine the relationship between the Voice of the Customer and FPL internal activities. To do this different customer groups are weighted, based on their size and usage of electricity. The fifth stage is to apply this weighting, ranked in importance with the 19 quality elements. In doing this, direct and indirect quality elements are combined; indirect elements correspond to those for organisations that represent and speak to the customer, such as a nuclear regulatory commission and the Florida Public Service Commission. Carrying on through this process they arrive at the overall ranking of the quality elements.

The next step is to prioritise FPL activities based on what quality elements the customer identified as the most important. This stage being complete, it is then summarised on to one large sheet of paper – the Table of Tables.

The FPL approach to the Table of Tables has been developed and fine-tuned over a considerable number of years. However, the approach of the Table of Tables does not have to be complicated. Florida Power and Light uses the Table of Tables to communicate the Voice of the Customer to all its employees. It is sent to every work location with instructions that it be set on the wall next to the bulletin boards, and in this way every employee can see what the customer thinks is important. FPL

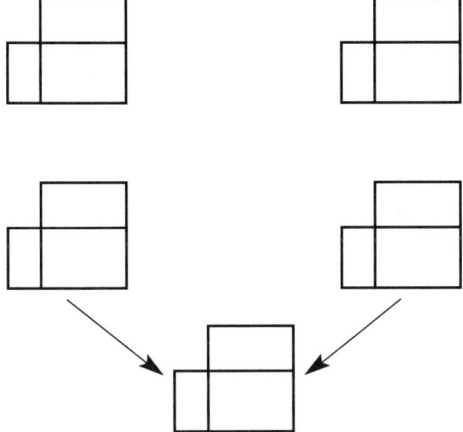

Figure 9.9   Table of Tables

has repeated this process on an annual basis.

An illustration of the approach of the Table of Tables is shown in Figure 9.9. Individual Houses of Quality for the different customer groups are weighted and combined to form a single Table of Tables, while still retaining the visual impact of the individual customer groups and what matters to them. We can also see what matters to the aggregate and how the individual Table of Tables contribute.

This approach could, of course, be extended to other stakeholders, as well as just customer groups, so that a Table of Tables might combine the interests of various stakeholders. This, however, would be more complex and is currently the subject of development activity for the team at Nottingham.

INTRODUCING BENCHMARKING INTO RESEARCH AND DEVELOPMENT

In the UK, interest in Benchmarking within R&D is a key feature of the activities of the TQM in R&D Study Group of the Quality Methods Association, of which Professor Bendell is

Chairperson. The TQM in R&D Study Group sees its mission as being to exchange ideas and practical experiences of Total Quality within R&D, and as part of this it has objectives to understand and provide opportunity to move to best practice, to provide a support network and forum for discussion of experiences, and to facilitate contacts on specific issues. The group has various activities, including regular meetings. Some of these meetings have concentrated specifically on the difficult subject of Benchmarking in R&D. At these meetings 'TQM users' from R&D in the UK have discussed their and their company's experiences of Benchmarking in the R&D area.

Dr Jim Crilley of Unilever Research describes the key to successful Benchmarking as 'recognising what is good, why it is good and how you are going to achieve it'. Product Benchmarking such as that practised by Chrysler in the 1960s, when they used it strip down every new Ford model, is just one form of Benchmarking. Equally useful, he says, can be the Benchmarking of strategies and expenditure in R&D. It follows from the definition of Benchmarking chosen by Dr Crilley – that of Shell 'the continuous process of measuring products, services and practices against the best competitors or those companies recognised as industry leaders' – that Benchmarking fundamentally involves measurement, for example of the number of design changes involved in taking a product to market.

Dr Crilley recommends four grades of Benchmarking:

1 Internal Benchmarking – 'better than we have done before';
2 Competitive Benchmarking – 'better than anyone in the industry';
3 Worldclass Benchmarking – 'better than anyone else';
4 Customer Benchmarking – 'better than our customers' expectations'.

Management has to recognise the level which it is seeking to achieve; if it is the world-class level then a Benchmarking team will be needed to be led by the owner of a process who will define and record key metrics.

Identification of the companies that you want to Benchmark against could be achieved, Dr Crilley suggests, by scanning literature, 'squeezing' information and by attending forum-type meetings. By looking at such literature you could 'tell a company's market entry strategy by the processes which they strongly emphasise'. 'Innovator' companies can be identified from the relative emphasis on people and innovation processes, while 'Imitator' companies are identifiable for their emphasis on planning and competitor-understanding processes.

In response to a question as to whether he knew of any examples of Benchmarking where the output was solely innovation, Dr Crilley has replied that innovation means lots of things to lots of people, but that one measure could be the number of patentable products produced. He cited the case of AT&T who have attempted to measure creativity, but found this much more difficult than the measurement of productivity.

Jim Clark of Research Machines, the micro-computer system manufacturers based in Oxford, reports that Benchmarking started in his company in the manufacturing sector in 1990 and had been extended to engineering later in that year.

Identification of best practices everywhere was central to this, and while it was the company's intention to Benchmark anything and everything, it was seen as important that too much was not collected all at once. It was recognised that Benchmarking can be an expensive exercise which should not be done for the fun of it, but rather as part of the normal improvement process. In the case of Research Machines, other computer companies were telling them a considerable amount about the personnel practices and engineering processes, although not their business processes. Rover Group had been particularly co-operative in the area of project management. Another area of interest was in knowing how other people are developing software – the languages that were being used, what the approaches were in checking and monitoring lines of code.

THE CREATIVE SERVICE SECTOR

Clearly, all management and service areas are candidates for quality improvement and Benchmarking, and a very good way forward, as in other areas, is to define the fundamental business processes, identify the appropriate basis for measurement and to seek excellence to Benchmark against. While the process is the same as elsewhere, the lack of definition and the problems of local attitudes can be severe. Where organisations are already certificated, or seeking certification, to BS 5750/ISO 9000, much of this process of definition and clarity of business processes would have begun to have been put in place. Where it is not yet at that stage, the cultural shock can be quite severe, although it is not uncommon in the service sector to find aspects of Competitor Benchmarking well established in business practice. Two examples of this are in magazine publishing, where review of the creative content of competitors' magazines, as well as advertising sales, is common and in the practices of London hotels which regularly provide one another with information on nightly or weekly occupancy figures and room yields. Such analyses do concentrate perhaps more on outputs than on process measures, but nevertheless provide the basis for genuine Benchmarking.

10 RELATIONSHIP TO INTERNATIONAL AWARD CRITERIA

INTRODUCTION

(Increased competitiveness, reduced cost and greater satisfaction among internal and external customers are but a few of the significant advantages from the implementation of a Total Quality Management (TQM) programme within an organisation. Realisation of this, coupled with the need to survive within an ever-increasing competitive market place has inevitably led to a change in attitude towards the internal structure within an organisation by senior management. It is not surprising, therefore, that many of the major business organisations in Europe have embarked on programmes to improve many of their management and business processes.)

This increase in the awareness of the commercial advantages that the implementation of Quality can bring to an organisation has led to a positive increase in its recognition. This recognition has taken the form of the presentation of various prestigious awards as acknowledgements of achievements in the field of Quality – indeed the criteria of the International Awards are in essence Benchmarks of Quality representing marks of excellence to be achieved. Indeed, even if organisations do not wish to enter for the awards, the criteria of the awards may still be used in a practicable way as a guidance for internal self-assessment.

SELF-ASSESSMENT AND BENCHMARKS

There is an increasing incentive for organisations to use the requirements of the International Awards as a means of evaluating their strengths and weaknesses on a structured basis for comparison with award winners and other organisations. Clearly, since award winners of prestigious awards such as the Deming Prize, the Malcolm Baldrige Award and the European Quality Award are, by definition, worldclass companies, undertaking such self-assessment is a genuine Benchmarking activity. (An example of an organisation which uses the Malcolm Baldrige Award criteria for Benchmarking its performance against on a corporate basis is IBM.) Further, the awards provide effective Benchmark Grids which, like the case of ISO 9000 mentioned in Chapter 1, provide a structured basis for the Benchmarking process.

These awards, some well established, some newcomers and others yet to be implemented, their background and their criteria are examined in this chapter.

THE DEMING PRIZE

Background

The Deming Prizes arose out of Dr Edward Deming's lectures in Japan on quality control in the 1950s. The Union of Japanese Scientists and Engineers established the Deming Prizes from royalties based on selling the lecture notes.

There are two prizes, the Deming Prize, for individuals who have made significant contributions to the dissemination and development of theories relating to Statistical Quality Control (SQC), and the Deming Application Prize, of which there are several different categories. This latter Prize is fundamentally a prize awarded to companies which, in any financial year, have performed significantly well in the area of SQC. In 1989, Florida Power and Light (FPL) became the first non-Japanese organisation to win the Deming Prize.

Assessment criteria

Ishikawa's checklist (1980) for the Deming Application Prize Criteria may be used by an organisation to check both their management and processes. A detailed list of criteria for the Prize is shown in Table 10.1.

Table 10.1   Ishikawa's Checklist of Criteria for the Deming Application Prize

CATEGORY EXAMINED	DEFINITION/EXPLANATION
1 Policy and objectives	Policy with regard to management, quality, and quality control Methods in determining policy and objectives Appropriateness and consistency of the contents of objectives Utilisation of statistical methods Dissemination and permeation of objectives Checking objectives and their implementations Relationships with long-range and short-range plans
2 Organisation and its operation	A clear-cut line of responsibilities Appropriateness of delegation of power Co-operation between divisions Activities of committees Utilisation of the staff Utilisation of Quality Control (QC) circle (small group) activities Quality control audit

CATEGORY EXAMINED	DEFINITION/EXPLANATION
3 Education and its dissemination	Education plan and actual accomplishment Conspicuousness about quality and control, understanding of quality control Education concerning statistical concepts and methods and a degree of permeation Ability to understand the effects Education for sub-contractors and outside organisations Quality Control circle (small group) activities Suggestion system
4 Assembling and disseminating information and its utilisation	Assembling outside information Disseminating information between divisions Speed in disseminating information (use of computer) (Statistical) analysis of information and its utilisation
5 Analysis	Selection of important problems and themes Appropriateness of the analytical method Utilisation of statistical methods Tying in with own engineering technology Quality analysis, process analysis Utilisation of results of analysis Positiveness of suggestions for improvement
6 Standardisation	System of standards Methods of establishing, revising and withdrawing standards Actual records in establishing, revising and withdrawing standards Contents of standards Utilisation of statistical methods Accumulation of technology Utilisation of standards
7 Control	Control systems for quality and related areas such as cost and quantity Control points and control items

CATEGORY EXAMINED	DEFINITION/EXPLANATION
7 Control (contd.)	Utilisation of statistical methods such as the control chart and general acceptance of the statistical way of thinking Contributions of Quality Control (QC) circle (small group) activities Actual conditions of control activities Actual conditions of control system
8 Quality assurance	Procedures for new product development Quality development (breakdown of quality function) and its analysis, reliability and design review Safety and product liability prevention Process control and improvement Process capabilities Measurement and inspection Control of facilities/equipment, sub-contracting, purchasing, services etc. Quality assurance system and its audit Utilisation of statistical methods Evaluation and audit of quality Practical conditions of quality assurance
9 Effects	Measuring effects Visibility effects, such as quality, serviceability, date of delivery, cost, profit, safety, environment etc. Invisible effects Compatibility between prediction of effects and actual records
10 Future plans	Understanding of the present conditions, and concreteness Policies adopted to solve shortcomings Plans of promotion for the future Relations with the company's long-range plans

THE MALCOLM BALDRIGE NATIONAL QUALITY AWARD

Background

In August 1987 President Reagan signed the Malcolm Baldrige Quality Act which officially established an annual US National Quality Award. This Award is developed and administered by the Secretary of Commerce and the National Institute of Standards and Technology (NIST), and the American Society for Quality Control (ASQC) assists in administering the Award Programme. It is primarily concerned with recognition of achievement improvement of quality, the establishment by an organisation of guidelines for self-evaluation and an expectancy that Award winners will allow others to share in their experiences, a factor which is illustrated by participation at senior management level at the annual Quest for Excellence Conference which is usually held two to three months after presentation of the award.

Past winners of the Award include, in 1988, in the manufacturing category of the award Motorola Inc., Westinghouse Commercial Nuclear Fuel Division, and in the Small Business Category, Globe Metallurgical Inc. In 1989, in the Manufacturing Category, Milliken & Company, Xerox Business Products and Systems were presented with awards. In 1990, in the Manufacturing Category of the Award, Cadillac Motor Car company and IBM, Rochester won an award, in the Service Category of the award in the same year Federal Express Corp. won an award and in the Small Business Category of the Award, Wallace Co. Inc. won an Award. In 1991, in the Manufacturing Category, Solectron Corp., and Zytec Corp. won Awards, and in the Small Business Category Marlow Industries won an award. In 1992, in the Manufacturing Division, AT&T Network Systems Group Transmission Systems Business Unit and Texas Instruments Inc., Defense Systems and Electronics

Group won awards, in the Service Category, AT&T Universal Card Services and The Ritz-Carlton Hotel Company won awards, and in the Small Business Category Granite Rock Company won an award.

Assessment criteria

Up to two Awards may be given each year, for organisations based in the USA, in the following categories;

- Large companies which are product based (manufacturing);
- Large companies which are service based;
- Smaller companies with less than 500 full-time employees.

The assessment criteria for 1993 consists of seven major categories which are then divided into separate examining areas. A point-scoring system exists for each of the major criteria with the maximum total being 1,000. A more in-depth analysis of the criteria may be seen in Table 10.2.

Table 10.2   Criteria and scoring for the 1993 Malcolm Baldrige Award

CATEGORY EXAMINED	DEFINITION/ EXPLANATION	POINTS
Leadership	Senior Executive Leadership	45
	Management for Quality	25
	Public Responsibility and Corporate Citizenship	25
Information and Analysis	Scope and Management of Quality and Performance Data and Information	15
	Competitive Comparisons and Benchmarking	20

CATEGORY EXAMINED	DEFINITION/ EXPLANATION	POINTS
Information and Analysis (contd.)	Analysis and Uses of Company-level Data	40
Strategic Quality Planning	Strategic Quality and Company Performance Planning Process	35
	Quality and Performance Plans	25
Human Resource Development and Management	Human Resource Planning and Management	20
	Employee Involvement	40
	Employee Education and Training	40
	Employee Performance and Recognition	25
	Employee Well-being and Satisfaction	25
Management of Process Quality	Design and Introduction of Quality Products and Services	40
	Process Management: Product and Service Production and Delivery Processes	35
	Process Management: Business Processes and Support Services	30
	Supplier Quality	20
	Quality Assessment	15
Quality and Operational Results	Product and Service Quality Results	70
	Company Operational Results	50
	Business Process and Support Service Results	25
	Supplier Quality Results	35

CATEGORY EXAMINED	DEFINITION/ EXPLANATION	POINTS
Customer Focus and Satisfaction	Customer Expectations: Current and Future	35
	Customer Relationship Management	65
	Commitment to Customers	15
	Customer Satisfaction Determination	30
	Customer Satisfaction Results	85
	Customer Satisfaction Comparison	70

THE EUROPEAN QUALITY AWARD

Background

In 1988, 14 of the leading Western European companies took the initiative of forming the European Foundation of Quality Management (EFQM). Their primary concern is enhancing the position of Western European organisations in the world market by stimulating and assisting the development of Quality Improvement activities, and by the acceleration of the acceptance of Quality as a strategy for global competitive advantage. It is this organisation, together with the support of the European Organisation for Quality and the European Commission, who sponsor the European Quality Award. The award is a relative newcomer to the scene, the first European Quality Award being presented in 1992 to Rank Xerox. In the same year European Quality Awards were awarded to BOC Special Gases, Industries del Ubierna SA, UBISA and Milliken European Division.

The European Quality Award for 1993 incorporates:

1 European Quality Prizes awarded to a number of companies that demonstrate excellence in the management of Quality as their fundamental process for continuous improvement; and
2 The European Quality Award which is awarded to the most successful exponent of Total Quality Management in Western Europe.

The first step in an application for the European Quality Award is the collation of a body of Quality Management data from within an organisation. This process is of significant value, for even if an organisation is not successful in winning the Award it will still enable them to assess their organisation's level of commitment to Total Quality Management and it will show them the extent to which commitment to Quality is being deployed throughout every level of the organisation. Applicants must provide information about the following areas of the business:

- History
- Organisation Chart
- Technology and raw materials
- Competitive environment
- Partnership arrangements
- Principal products and services
- Customer and supplier base
- Regulatory environment
- Key product/service quality factors
- Other important factors.

Assessment criteria

There are two essential aspects of the European Assessment Model, in Figure 10.1. These are ENABLERS which concern the assessment criteria in relation to how results are being achieved and the RESULTS which are concerned with the assessment criteria in relation to what the organisation has achieved and is achieving. In accordance with the European

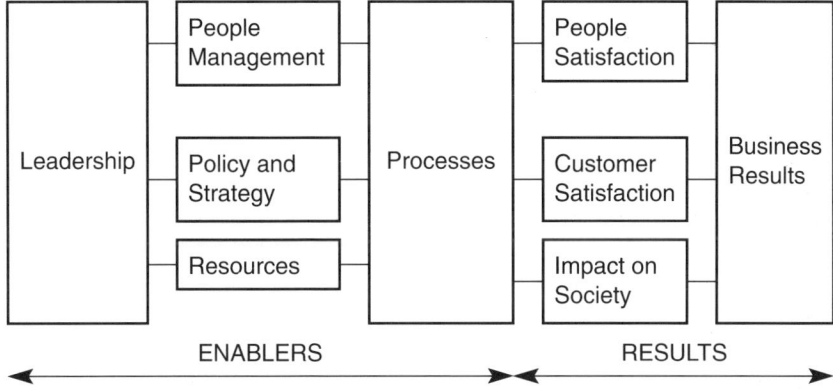

Figure 10.1 European Total Quality Management Model

model processes are the means by which the organisation harnesses and releases the talents of its people to produce results. Therefore, the processes and the people are the enablers which provide the results.

The model, Figure 10.1, was developed as a framework for the European Quality Award. It informs us that:

- Customer Satisfaction, People (employee) Satisfaction and Impact on Society are achieved through
- Leadership driving
- Policy and strategy, People Management, Resources and Processes, leading ultimately to excellence in
- Business Results.

The nine major categories of assessment criteria are shown in Figure 10.1 and detailed in Table 10.3 for the Enablers.

Enablers

Table 10.3 gives an explanation of the various Enablers as they contribute to the European Model for self-appraisal and in Figure 10.2 the criteria against which they will be scored are detailed.

1 The degree of excellence of your approach 2 The degree of deployment of your approach		
Anecdotal or non-value adding	0%	Little effective usage
Some evidence of soundly based approaches and prevention based systems Subject to occasional review Some area of integration into normal operations	25%	Applied to about one-quarter of the potential when considering all relevant areas and activities
Evidence of soundly based systematic approaches and prevention based systems Subject to regular review with respect to business effectiveness Integration into normal operations and planning well established	50%	Applied to about half the potential when considering all relevant areas and activities
Clear evidence of soundly based systematic approaches and prevention based systems Clear evidence of refinement and improvement business effectiveness through review cycles Good integration into normal operations and planning well established	75%	Applied to about three-quarters of the potential when considering all relevant areas and activities
Clear evidence of soundly based systematic approaches and prevention based systems Clear evidence of refinement and improvement business effectiveness through review cycles Approach has become totally integrated into normal working patterns Could be used as a role model for other organisations	100%	Applied to full potential when considering all relevant areas and activities

Figure 10.2   Criteria for Scoring Enablers

Table 10.3 European Quality Award Assessment Criteria for Enablers 1

CATEGORY	DEFINITION/EXPLANATION
1 Leadership **100 Points**	The behaviour of all managers in driving the organisation towards Total Quality. How the executive team and all other managers inspire and drive Total Quality as the organisation's fundamental process for continuous improvement. Evidence is needed of:
	1(a) Visible involvement in leading Total Quality Areas to address could include how managers take positive step to: ● communicate with staff ● act as role models leading by example ● make themselves accessible and listen to staff ● give and receive training ● demonstrate commitment to Total Quality
	1(b) A consistent Total Quality culture Areas to address could include how managers take positive steps to: ● be involved in assessing awareness of Total Quality ● be involved in reviewing progress in Total Quality ● include commitment to and achievement in Total Quality in appraisal and promotion of staff at all levels
	1(c) Timely recognition and appreciation of the efforts and successes of individual and teams Areas to address could include how managers are involved in recognition ● at local ● at division ● at organisational level

CATEGORY	DEFINITION/EXPLANATION
1 Leadership **100 Points** **(contd.)**	● of groups outside the organisation, e.g. suppliers or customers
	1(d) Support of Total Quality by provision of appropriate resources and assistance Areas to address could include how managers provide support through: ● funding learning ● funding facilitation ● funding improvement activity ● funding those taking initiatives ● funding championing a cause ● helping to define priorities in improvement activity
	1(e) Involvement with customers and suppliers Areas to address could include how managers take positive steps to ● meet customers and suppliers ● establish and participate in 'partnership' relationships – with customers and suppliers ● establish and participate in joint improvement teams with customers and suppliers
	1(f) Active promotion of Total Quality outside the organisation Areas to address could include how managers promote quality management outside the organisation through ● membership of professional bodies ● publication of booklets, articles ● presentations at conferences, seminars etc. ● assistance to local community
2 Policy and Strategy **80 Points**	The organisation's mission, values, vision and strategic direction and the ways in which the organisation achieves them. How the company's policy and strategy

CATEGORY	DEFINITION/EXPLANATION
2 Policy and Strategy **80 Points** **(contd.)**	reflects the concept of Total Quality and how the principles of Total Quality are used in the determination, deployment, review and improvement of policy and strategy. Evidence is needed of:
	2(a) How policy and strategy are based on the concept of Total Quality Areas to address could include how Total Quality is reflected in the organisation's: ● values ● vision ● mission statement ● strategy statements
	2(b) How policy and strategy are formed on the basis of information that is relevant to Total Quality Areas to address could include how use is made of: ● feedback from customers and suppliers ● feedback from the organisation's people ● data on performance of competitors and 'best in class' organisations ● data on social issues ● data on regulatory and legislative issues
	2(c) How policy and strategy are the basis of business plans Areas to address could include how: ● business plans are tested, evaluated, improved and aligned with the organisation's policy
	2(d) How policy and strategy are communicated Areas to address could include how: ● newsletters, posters, videos etc. are used

CATEGORY	DEFINITION/EXPLANATION
2 Policy and Strategy 80 Points (contd.)	• communications on policy are planned and prioritised • the organisation evaluates the awareness of people to its policy
	2(e) How policy and strategy are regularly reviewed and improved Areas to address could include how: • the organisation evaluates the effectiveness and relevance of its policy • the organisation reviews and improves its policy
3 People Management 90 Points	The management of the organisation's people. How the organisation releases the full potential of its people to improve its business continously. Evidence is needed of:
	3(a) How continuous improvement in people management is accomplished Areas to address could include how: • people management is reviewed and improved • the human resources strategy plan supports the company's policy and strategy • surveys of perceptions of the organisation's people are used
	3(b) How the skills and capabilities of the people are preserved and developed through recruitment, training and career progression Areas to address could include how: • people's skills are defined and compared with the organisation's requirements • recruitment and advancement are planned • training plans are established and implemented

CATEGORY	DEFINITION/EXPLANATION
3 People Management **90 Points** **(contd.)**	• the effectiveness of training is reviewed • people are developed following initial training
	3(c) How people and terms agree targets and continuously review performance Areas could include how: • objectives of individuals and teams are negotiated • people are appraised
	3(d) How the involvement of everyone in continuous improvement is promoted and people are empowered to take appropriate action Areas to address could include how: • suggestion schemes are used • use is made of teams of quality improvement • in-house conferences and meetings are used • people are empowered to take action
	3(e) How effective top-down and bottom-up communication is achieved Address to address could include how: • regular two-way briefing meetings are used • the organisation keeps in touch with its people • the organisation transmits information to its people
4 Resources **90 Points**	The management, utilisation and preservation of resources. How the organisation's resources are effectively deployed in support of policy and strategy. Evidence is needed of how business improvements are achieved continuously by management of:

CATEGORY	DEFINITION/EXPLANATION
4 Resources **90 Points** **(contd.)**	**4(a) Financial resources** Areas to address could include how: ● cash flow and balance sheet elements are managed ● financial strategies reflect Total Quality ● shareholder value is managed ● criteria for financial decision-making support for Total Quality ● 'quality cost' concepts are used
	4(b) Information resources Areas to address could include how: ● information systems are managed ● information validity, integrity, security and scope are assured and improved ● information to customers, suppliers and people involved in improvement is made more accessible ● information strategies support Total Quality
	4(c) Material resources Areas to address could include how: ● raw material sources and supplies are managed ● material inventories are optimised ● material waste is minimised ● fixed assets are utilised to optimum effect
	4(d) Application of Technology Areas could include how: ● alternative and emerging technologies are identified and evaluated according to their impact on the business ● technology has been exploited to secure competitive advantage ● the development of people's skills and capabilities is harmonised with the development of technology ● technology is harnessed in support of

CATEGORY	DEFINITION/EXPLANATION
4 Resources **90 Points** **(contd.)**	improvements in processes and information systems and other systems • intellectual property is protected and exploited
5 Processes **140 Points**	The management of all the value-adding activities within the organisation. How the processes are identified, reviewed and if necessary revised to ensure continuous improvement of the organisation's business. Self-appraisal should indicate:
	5(a) How processes critical to the success of the organisation are identified Areas to address could include how: • critical processes are defined: what processes are currently on the list • the method of identification is conducted • interface issues are resolved • 'impact on the business' is evaluated Critical processes could include: • provision of raw materials and supplies • manufacturing • engineering • reception of orders • delivery of product or service • invoicing and collection of debt • determining of customer and people satisfaction • design • new product and service development • budgeting and planning • management of safety, health, environment
	5(b) How the organisation systematically manages its processes Areas to be addressed could include how:

CATEGORY	DEFINITION/EXPLANATION
5 Processes **140 Points** **(contd.)**	• process ownership and standards of operation are established • standards are monitored and by whom • performance measures are used in process management • quality systems standards, e.g. ISO 900 are applied in process management
	5(c) How process performance measurements, along with all relevant feedback are used to review processes and to set targets for improvements Areas to address could include how: • feedback from people, customers, suppliers and data from Benchmarking are used in setting standards of operation and targets for improvement • current performance measurements and targets for improvement are related to past achievement • the processes critical to the success of the business are reviewed • challenging targets are identified and used
	5(d) How the organisation stimulates innovation and creativity in process improvement Areas to address could include how: • new principles of design, new technology and new operating philosophies are discovered and utilised • the creative talents of employees are brought to bear
	5(e) How the organisation implements process changes and evaluates the benefits Areas to address could include how:

CATEGORY	DEFINITION/EXPLANATION
5 Processes **140 Points** **(contd.)**	• new or changed processes are piloted and implementation controlled • process changes are communicated and to whom • staff are trained prior to implementation • process changes are audited to ensure predicated results are achieved

Results

Just as Enablers are scored, results can be similarly measured against the criteria given in Figure 10.3.

1 The degree of excellence of your results 2 The scope of your results		
Anecdotal	0%	Results address few relevant areas and activities
On balance a positive trend Some satisfactory results	25%	Results address some relevant areas and activities
Strongly positive trend Good results in most areas Negative trends/results understood and have been addressed with well-defined corrective/prevention action plans	50%	Results address many relevant areas and activities
Strongly positive trend Good results in most areas Negative trends/results understood and have been addressed with well-defined corrective/prevention action plans	75%	Results address most relevant areas and activities
Excellent, 'best in class' results and strongly positive trends Sustained performance Positive indication that leading position will be maintained	100%	Results address all relevant areas and facets of the organisation

Figure 10.3   Criteria for Scoring Results

The results criteria are divided into four sections as detailed in Table 10.4.

These are:

- customer satisfaction;
- people satisfaction;
- impact on society;
- business results.

They are concerned with what the organisation has achieved and is achieving. These can be expressed as discrete results, but ideally as trend over a period of years.

The organisation's results and trends for each results criterion should be addressed in terms of:

1 a company's actual performance;
2 a company's own targets, and, wherever possible;
3 the performance competitors;
4 the performance of 'best in class' organisations.

Self-appraisal should indicate the extent to which the organisation's activities are covered by, and the relative importance of, the parameters chosen to measure results.

Table 10.4 European Quality Award Assessment Criteria for Enablers 2

CATEGORY EXAMINED	DEFINITION/EXPLANATION
6 Customer Satisfaction **200 Points**	What the perception of external customers is of the organisation and of its products and services. Evidence is needed of the companies' success in satisfying the needs and expectations of customers.
	Areas to address could include customers' perceptions of the organisation with respect to: Product and service quality: • capability of meeting specifications • defect, error, rejection rates • consistency, reproducibility

CATEGORY EXAMINED	DEFINITION/EXPLANATION
6 Customer Satisfaction **200 Points** **(contd.)**	● maintainability ● durability ● reliability ● on-time delivery ● in-full delivery ● logistics information ● delivery frequency ● responsiveness and flexibility ● product availability ● accessibility of key staff ● production training and sales support ● production literature ● technical support ● simplicity, convenience and accuracy of documentation ● awareness of customer problems ● complaint handling ● warranty and guarantee provisions ● spare part availability ● innovation in service quality ● product development ● payment terms and financing
	Additional indications of customer satisfaction could include: ● complaint levels customer returns (by value and quantity) ● warranty payments ● rework levels ● accolades and awards received
7 People Satisfaction **90 Points**	What the people's feelings are about their organisation. Evidence is needed of companies success in satisfying the needs and expectations of its people. Areas to address could include people's perceptions of the organisation with respect to: ● working environment; location, space, amenities ● health and safety provisions

CATEGORY EXAMINED	DEFINITION/EXPLANATION
7 People Satisfaction **90 Points** **(contd.)**	• communication at local and organisation level • appraisal, target setting and career planning • training, development; retraining • awareness of requirements of job • awareness of organisation values, vision and strategy • awareness of Total Quality process • involvement in Total Quality process • recognition schemes • reward schemes • organisation (line management) • organisation for Total Quality • management style • job security Additional indicators of people satisfaction could include: • absenteeism and sickness • staff turnover • ease of recruitment • grievances • use of company-provided facilities
8 Impact on Society **60 Points**	What the perception of the organisation is among society at large. This includes views of the organisation's approach to quality of life, the environment and to the preservation of global resources. Evident is needed of the company's success in satisfying the needs and expectations of the community at large.
	Areas to address could include perceptions of the local and wider community with respect to the following: The organisation's active involvement in the community in terms of: • charity • education and training • medical and welfare • sports and leisure

CATEGORY EXAMINED	DEFINITION/EXPLANATION
8 Impact on Society **60 Points** **(contd.)**	The organisation's activities to reduce and prevent nuisance and harm to neighbours as a result of operations, business-related transportation and products in terms of: • effluent and pollutions • hazards • noise • health risks The organisation's activities to assist the preservation of global resources in terms of: • energy conservation • usage of raw materials and other inputs • usage of recycled materials • reduction of waste • environment and ecology Additional indications of impact on society could include: • number of general complaints • number of infringements of national and international standards • accolades and awards received by the organisation • effect of employment instability
9 Business Results **150 Points**	What the organisation is achieving in relation to its planned business performance. Evidence is needed of the company's continuing success in achieving its financial and other business targets and objectives, and in satisfying the needs and expectations of everyone with a financial interest in the company. There is a need to demonstrate that the company's business plan is sound.
	Financial measures Areas to address could include some of the following: • profit • cash flow • sales

CATEGORY EXAMINED	DEFINITION/EXPLANATION
9 Business Results **150 Points** **(contd.)**	● value added ● working capital ● liquidity ● shareholder returns ● long-term 'value for shareholders'
	Non-financial measures These will relate to achievement of other critical business targets and objectives, and will include internal efficiency and effectiveness measures that are vital to the organisation's continuing success. Areas to address could include some of the following: ● market share ● waste ● defects per unit of output or activity ● variability of product or service ● cost on non-quality ● service level achievements In addition cycle times could be addressed such as: ● order processing time ● product delivery time ● batch processing time ● time to bring new products and services to the market ● time to break-even on new development ● inventory turnover time

THE BRITISH QUALITY AWARD

Background

The British Quality Award, launched in 1984 by the British Quality Association (BQA) which has now become the British Quality Fundation (BQF), was introduced to encourage Total

Quality in industrial and corporate organisations based in Britain. The awards are presented annually to individuals and groups which have significantly improved the standard of quality of a product, process or service.

Assessment Criteria

The judges look for a significant improvement in Quality in the last four years. This relates to input product design and/or manufacture or planning and/or operation of a service, or development and/or operation of a process. Its criteria are not as detailed as the Baldrige Award and the scoring system is not made public.

In 1992 a Quality Award Committee was set up at the request of the Secretary of State for Trade and Industry at the time, Peter Lilley. The objective of this committee was to consider the feasibility of developing an award specifically related to British business.

Both the objectives of the Malcolm Baldrige and the European Quality Awards were taken into consideration by the committee which eventually arrived at the conclusion that the objective of a new British Quality Award would be:

> To increase the penetration of a high level of Total Quality Management awareness and practices on a significant and progressive scale through UK business.

BENCHMARKING AWARDS

Background

The International Benchmarking Clearing House, a service of the American Productivity and Quality Centre (APQC), based in Houston, Texas and founded in 1977 has recently announced the creation of a new set of awards, the Benchmarking Awards.

The three separate awards, consisting of the Benchmarking Research Prize, the Benchmarking Study Prize and the Award for Excellence in Benchmarking, illustrate the increasing significance of Benchmarking in the commercial environment.

The Benchmarking Research Prize

The primary purpose of the Benchmarking Research Prize is the extension of Benchmarking knowledge. This is seen as being carried out by methods such as original contributions to the development of tools for Benchmarking and research into techniques for Benchmarking.

There are two categories of this Award; academic research and applied research, and in each of these two categories up to two awards may be made per annum.

The 1992 Benchmarking Research Prize criteria concentrate on the more technical aspects of Benchmarking by encouraging and seeking out contributions in data collection, analysis and integration of Benchmarking techniques; the underlying purpose being one of reinforcing the increased usage of statistical techniques and managerial tools in Benchmarking.

The Award is only open to those individuals or teams which have an association with colleges, universities or non-profit-making educational institutions.

The Benchmarking Study Prize

The primary purpose of this award is the recognition of excellence in the execution of a Benchmarking Study.

According to the 1992 Benchmarking Study Prize criteria applicants, who may be teams or individuals, must demonstrate and document their process for conducting a Benchmarking project. The following areas must all be addressed by applicants:

- The rationale for selecting the project;
- The process used in Benchmarking;
- The Benchmarking study plan and team responsibilities;
- The Benchmarking questionnaire and results of secondary research;
- The results and conclusions of the study;
- The action plan recommended to management;
- The results achieved.

Evaluation of applicants is based on their approach, the quality of analysis and execution of the study, and the results obtained for the study. The project must also be endorsed by a project sponsor or management representative who is required to testify to the importance of the study.

Award for Excellence in Benchmarking

The primary purpose of this Award is the recognition of an organisation's demonstration of consistent application of Benchmarking.

There are five different categories. A detailed account of the criteria for 1992 is shown in Table 10.5. Note that the detailed criteria are subject to change for 1993.

Table 10.5   Award for Excellence in Benchmarking Criteria

CATEGORY	DEFINITION/EXPLANATION
Category 1 **Strategic Planning** **Integration and** **Information** **Structure** **(225 points)**	This category examines the integration of Benchmarking with the organisation's planning process, and how the scope, sources and uses of Benchmarking information are integrated into improvement activities. Also examined is senior management involvement and how goals, plans and strategies are developed based on competitive information and the application of Benchmarks.

CATEGORY	DEFINITION/EXPLANATION
A Strategic Planning Integration	
35 Points	Existence of company planning documents that indicate a structured plan for Benchmarking which is linked with company planning guidelines and targeted to improving performance in quality and customer satisfaction, cycle time, productivity cost of key business processes and support activities.
25 Points	Activities of executives in establishing Benchmarking topics and determining key Benchmarking partnerships; activities of senior managers in supporting Benchmarking activities, participating in Benchmarking studies and reviewing Benchmarking study results
20 Points (each)	How Benchmarking is integrated into other improvement activities. How the organisation develops goals, plans and strategies based upon projection of the competitive environment and application of benchmarks
15 Points	Criteria for both seeking benchmarks and identifying potential Benchmarking partners
B Information Structure	
30 Points	The scope, sources and uses of Benchmarking information, including but not limited to the following: (a) Customer satisfaction and other customer data (b) Product/Service quality (c) Internal operations including business processes, support services and employee satisfaction

CATEGORY	DEFINITION/EXPLANATION
B Information Structure (contd.) 30 Points (contd.)	(d) Financial performance for overhead management, inventory management, debt management, cost of sales etc. (e) Environment, safety and health considerations of the business (f) Supplier performance
25 Points	Process for integrating Benchmarking data with other competitive, market and customer data in order to determine what to Benchmark
20 Points	How Benchmarking is used to encourage new ideas and improve the understanding of key business processes
20 Points	How the organisation evaluates and improves the scope, sources and uses of Benchmarking data
15 Points	How the organisation decides when to compare within and outside of its industry
Category 2 **Benchmarking Process** **and Support Structure** **(250 points)**	This category examines the linkage of the Benchmarking process, improvement activities, resource allocation and the deployment of training. Also examined is the adequacy of the company's support structure, including organisational structure, information repository, tracking and review process for Benchmarking studies
A Benchmarking Process	
35 Points	The linkage of the Benchmarking process to the company's planning process and other improvement activities and how resource allocation is considered for improvements indicated as the result of Benchmarking studies

CATEGORY	DEFINITION/EXPLANATION
A Benchmarking Process (contd.)	
30 Points	The Benchmarking process and model used by the organisation.
30 Points	Data repository for Benchmarking plans, questionnaires, studies, and reports. How this repository is developed by employees and how it is kept current
20 Points	The method for tracking the progress and completion of individual Benchmarking projects
22 Points	The review process for proposed Benchmarking studies (either internally or externally proposed) to assure appropriate legal and management considerations. The review process for assuring appropriate management participation
15 Points	The application of the Benchmarking Code of Conduct and how it is disseminated to Benchmarking teams
B Support Structure	
35 Points	Criteria for conducting formal training in Benchmarking and the extent of the deployment of Benchmarking training for categories of employees (supervising or sponsoring manager, Benchmarking facilitator, team leader, team member etc)
20 Points	Organisation structure and job responsibilities for individuals supporting Benchmarking
20 Points	How Benchmarking efforts are co-ordinated to eliminate redundancy of team efforts and to ensure that key Benchmarks are refreshed periodically

CATEGORY	DEFINITION/EXPLANATION
B Support Structure (contd.)	
25 Points	Organisation procedures for communicating Benchmarking activities and for providing opportunities for Benchmarking study teams to meet and share information about their process
Category 3 (125 points) Teamwork and Employee Involvement	This category examines the involvement of process owner, employees, and other stakeholders in Benchmarking studies; the selection, roles and responsibilities of team members; and how internal Benchmarking expertise is deployed to support the teams. Also examined are how teams are recognised, and how Benchmarking study teams communicate their Benchmarking activities
25 Points	How cross-functional and cross-divisional needs are considered during Benchmarking studies and how these concerns are institutionalised in the company's Benchmarking process
15 Points	How process owners and process stakeholders are involved in Benchmarking study projects
20 Points	The selection criteria for Benchmarking teams and the roles and responsibilities of team members
15 Points	How time and resources are allocated to Benchmarking teams
15 Points	The relationship of Benchmarking team membership to the implementation team members who will pursue the recommended action plans
20 Points	How the organisation uses its employees with Benchmarking expertise to coach, mentor, support or lead study teams
15 Points	How the organisation recognises employees for participating in Benchmarking activities

CATEGORY	DEFINITION/EXPLANATION
Category 4 **Business Alliances and Networking** **(100 points)**	This category examines how an organisation defines, establishes, manages and promotes alliances and partnerships including professional societies, trade associations and quality-focused organisations to support Benchmarking activities. Also included are how the organisation uses research, competitive information, consultants, suppliers, major accounts and common interest groups to address specific Benchmarking topics
25 Points	How Benchmarking alliances and partnerships are established and the rationale used for the selection of those organisations targeted for special relationships
25 Points	How the organisation uses membership in quality-focused and Benchmarking organisations, and professional societies and trade associations to support its Benchmarking efforts
25 Points	How the organisation uses its suppliers and major accounts to support its Benchmarking efforts
25 Points	How the organisation forms common interest groups to address specific Benchmarking topics
Category 5 **Results and improvement in Benchmarked processes** **(300 points)**	The results and improvements in Benchmarked processes category examines the specific Benchmarks that have been identified and monitored over the past three years, and evidence of the use of Benchmarking to improve these processes Applicants should indicate evidence of Benchmarks, process goals established and results tracked to goals to indicate trends in improvement. (The results may be normalised or indexed to protect

CATEGORY	DEFINITION/EXPLANATION
Category 5 **Results and improvement** **in Benchmarked processes** **(300 points)** **(contd.)**	proprietary information.) The frequency of recalibration of benchmarks should be indicated and the criteria for recycling studies should be discussed. Evidence submitted could include, but is not limited to, a discussion of the following
50 Points	What key measure and indicators the organisation uses to evaluate and improve its Benchmarking process (cycle time, access time to result and integration of customer, market financial and operational Benchmarking data)
50 Points	How the organisation determines objectivity and validity in the results of Benchmarking studies
200 Points	Current levels and trends in the performance of Benchmarked processes in comparison to prebenchmarked activities. Specific benchmarks, indicators and measures used by the organisation should be appropriate to the Benchmarking process. Benchmarks could include, but are not limited to, the following *Customer Satisfaction* (segmented by customer group as appropriate) Customer reject rates Customer satisfaction levels On-time delivery Customer loss/gain Market share loss/gain Other measures of responsiveness to customers *Quality and Productivity* Defector error rates First pass yield Equipment downtime Rework costs Warranty costs as a percentage of sales revenue

CATEGORY	DEFINITION/EXPLANATION
Category 5 **Results and improvement** **in Benchmarked** **processes** **(300 points)** 200 Points (contd.)	Number of engineering change orders Labour productivity Inventory turnover Resource utilisation *Cycle-time* Time-to-market for new products Cycle time for key business processes *Employee well-being and morale* Employee satisfaction Safety Absenteeism Turnover Employee training and development Employee recognition *Environmental impact*

11 FIGHTING YOUR WAY THROUGH THE HYPE – SOME SIMPLE 'DO'S' AND 'DON'TS'

INTRODUCTION

This chapter considers some of the simple 'do's' and 'don'ts' in relation to successful Benchmarking. It does not attempt to suggest that there is an A–Z dictionary for successful Benchmarking. Note that the points are neither given in order of importance or in order of conduct. However, it does examine some of the fundamental issues to be considered by organisations, before, during and after embarking upon a Benchmarking initiative within an organisation.

DOES A PERFORMANCE GAP EXIST IN YOUR ORGANISATION?

A genuine loss of monetary profit within an organisation is no joke, but in an ever-increasing competitive market place it is unfortunately, for many organisations, becoming all too common place. This identification of loss of profits is merely the first step, proceeding the following questions.

- Why has this happened?
- What is the difference between a successful competitor's performance and our own?
- Who are the best performers in relation to what we do? and

- What do we do about improving our own performance?

All need to be considered. Identification of a performance gap is then merely the first step. Improvement of performance and how an organisation sets about increasing their share in the commercial world is the next.

COMMITMENT FROM THE TOP

One of the most desirable factors for stimulating and encouraging a Benchmarking initiative within an organisation is top/ senior executive commitment and responsibility. It is therefore essential that once a decision has been taken to embark upon a new business strategy that commitment from the top may be relied upon. This sort of commitment may be engendered from the beginning in terms of training and education as to what Benchmarking is, how it can be utilised for the good of the organisation and how to implement those changes within the organisation.

The need for change within an organisation is usually identified by senior management. However, once identification of a performance gap has been made and a positive approach to implementation of a new initiative has taken place it will not be effective unless the whole of the workforce sees a positive commitment from within the top ranks of the organisation. Management should be active members of the Benchmarking team; this ensures their responsibility for the project. A Benchmarking initiative must be planned and, as with other major programmes of change, there must be a company policy in relation to it. This ensures continuity and clarity for those people in the Benchmarking team, as well as those outside the Benchmarking team.

Activity must be steered and reviewed if the organisation is to receive benefits from the initiative. The only way that this may be accomplished is if management take responsibility for the Benchmarking initiative. It follows from this that the right things are done at the right time and in the best interests of the company. Top management must therefore be responsible for continuity, commitment, policy objectives and the direction which the Benchmarking initiative will take. If positive improvements are to take place within an organisation, Benchmarking must be taken 'seriously' by all those involved.

As with any new organisational strategy there must be an underlying belief in the need for the change. If there is a positive belief in the need for change from within an organisation, then something worthwhile will eventually be accomplished. It is essential therefore for management to generate an ongoing, continuous enthusiasm for changes within the organisation and for the initiatives which are responsible for bringing those changes.

The importance of top management commitment is illustrated by the recent survey conducted by the American Productivity Center in the US. According to this survey, top management commitment emerges as being the most important factor for driving a Benchmarking initiative throughout an organisation. Lack of support from management can have a negative effect on Benchmarking and is, according to the survey, seen as a contributory factor to unsuccessful Benchmarking projects within organisations.

THE BENCHMARKING TEAM

Benchmarking is a real team effort and a team approach should be taken. However, it is always practical to have one or maybe two people who will act as facilitator(s) for the team. Of course, the involvement of a facilitator will depend upon the individual personalities of the team. Some organisations prefer to have a full-time facilitator for the team while others use the teamwork process as a means of self-facilitation.

The individual team members should consist of those people who are directly responsible for the processes which are to be Benchmarked – the process owners, with perhaps also representatives from within those departments which the Benchmarking exercises directly effect.

'FLAVOUR OF THE MONTH' SYNDROME

All too often organisations will suffer from the 'flavour of the month' syndrome, that is where organisations look for quick solutions to what are essentially long-term problems. Benchmarking is not a quick fix to long-term problems and should not been seen as such; if it is then you will be disappointed. The results from Benchmarking may not be initially easily identifiable. Therefore if you do choose to Benchmark, do not expect a quick fix in relation to problems.

COMBINE BENCHMARKING WITH OTHER TOTAL QUALITY INITIATIVES – BENCHMARKING MUST BE COME PART OF THE OVERALL STRATEGY

To be effective Benchmarking must become part of the regular management agenda, more than that, it should become part of organisational strategy. Benchmarking is a natural progression of Total Quality Management (TQM). The two should be combined, for they are both supportive of and complimentary to each other. The aim is to establish a Benchmarking initiative as an ongoing process with full integration into the organisational structure. Establishment of best practice within an organisation, after a while, becomes the natural way of doing things.

INTERNAL BUSINESS PROCESSES

Before embarking on any new management initiative it is essential that you become familiar with your own internal business processes. In fact, knowledge of an organisation's internal business processes is cited by the US survey, as being one of the most important factors for Benchmarking with 98 per cent of organisations which took part in the survey seeing this factor as being of 'great' or 'very great' importance to a successful study. A major part of this is understanding what the Critical Success Factors in your company are, i.e. those factors upon which the success or the failure of the organisation can be measured. If you do not know what they are, then it naturally follows that you will not know which processes to Benchmark.

Familiarisation with an organisation's internal processes may take anything between six months and a year dependent, of course, on how large the organisation is. One of the pitfalls is not following this process through thoroughly. This can result in the Benchmarking team arranging an external visit to collect information before they are actually ready to make the best use of the visit. These visits result in frustration, with management obtaining data which are of no relevance to their own organisation – a needless, wasteful and disappointing journey.

WHICH INTERNAL PROCESSES ARE TO BE BENCHMARKED?

Familiarisation with important internal processes is the key to understanding which of the internal processes are to be Benchmarked. Any activity within an organisation that can be measured can be Benchmarked, this means that both functional and generic processes may be Benchmarked.

Functional Benchmarking involves a comparison with those organisations which are not direct competitors – but who do carry out similar functional activities to one's own organisation. The advantages of functional Benchmarking are many – it is easy to identify similar functional areas in many organisations and confidentiality is not usually an issue, making the exchange of data between organisations considerably easier. Generic Benchmarking may be defined as the Benchmarking of those business processes which cut across various functions but in quite different industries. The advantage of this is that the various approaches to processes in different industries are likely to be most diverse, creating the most innovative break-throughs for improvement within an organisation. However, it follows that the processes to be Benchmarked will be those which the organisation depends upon to survive in the commercial environment.

While any activity can be measured and consequently Benchmarked, most companies will start with those areas where they know they need to be competitive to remain in business. The company should have a clear mission statement or list of business goals which is used to focus improvement activity. Customer satisfaction is high on most company priority lists, as is the need for a low cost operation. Deciding these broad areas partly answers the question, where do we want to be? These broad areas, however, need to be broken down into more specific activities that can be measured. What are the processes that deliver customer satisfaction? Which processes eat up the costs? The more precisely you define what you need to measure, the more useful will be the information that you gather to compare it with. What things are important to customers? What will help them to be successful? How good is the service currently given? etc.

CARRY OUT RESEARCH INTO BENCHMARKING

Benchmarking must be centred around planned research, inclusive of both internal and external sources. As a direct consequence of the Benchmarking Boom there has been a significant increase in information in relation to this subject, which in turn has made Benchmarking information more accessible.

The starting point is the collection of material from within your own organisation. Perhaps another part of the organisation has carried out Benchmarking before – find out before you start researching into external sources. Internal information is always useful, it is relevant to what your organisation does.

Information from the external customers is also useful. What do they think is the most important process in your organisation? Contacts within the same business are also useful; if they have carried out successful Benchmarking initiatives they might be willing to share information. Consultants, academics and industrial observers are all relevant sources of information. All of these sources should be supplemented by data obtained from business literature, that is periodicals, TQM magazines, trade journals and material available in libraries, and from Benchmarking conferences/workshops, seminars, annual reports, public databases, research institutions and Government agencies.

CHOICE OF PARTNER

A good way of choosing a partner is to start by listing those processes which are considered to be essential to the survival of the organisation and then asking the question 'who, or what, is better than us?'

When looking for an appropriate partner do not dismiss

internal choices, i.e. those from within your own organisation. Where an organisation is large and there are different sites in different regions then internal comparisons can be successfully made which may result in improved performance. It is very easy to make internal comparisons between departments, sites or even companies within the same group. The advantage here is that exchanges of information may not be covered by strict confidentiality agreements and that no direct competition is involved, making information inaccessible. In addition to this, the organisations may share the same politics, ethics, culture, language etc., all of which make the process more simple. Visits are straightforward to arrange and information is readily available to make use of. Operations are often very similar across sites and so Benchmarking these activities is considerably easier then Benchmarking processes in an external organisation.

A choice of an internal partner may effectively cut across many barriers, however, the real improvements within an organisation come from comparisons with external partners. External partners may either be found in other businesses which are part of the same group or they may be selected regardless of business, industry sector or location as best practice partners.

Remember that a choice of an external partner is far more difficult. Benchmarking visits to competitors will, by their very nature, be surrounded by confidentiality. However, the best way to organise a visit to a competitor is by both organisations agreeing before the visit to sign confidentiality agreements/ mutual non-disclosure agreements as to what material will be exchanged in relation to success and best practice. This will, hopefully, avoid misunderstandings between the organisations and open up a channel of communication for the future. Of course, company reports are always a useful way of looking at another organisation's performance.

VISITING THE PARTNER TO BE BENCHMARKED

Once a partner for the Benchmarking activity has been chosen, decide before the visit exactly what it is you are trying to achieve from the visit. The Benchmarking team must be fully conversant with the purpose of the visit, as should the partner you have chosen to Benchmark. Questionnaires should already have been sent to the proposed Benchmarking partner, in addition to communicating your expectations from the session with the partner. Perhaps one of the best ways of accomplishing this is to send them an agenda setting out what you expect to cover during the time you are at their organisation.

It is also important to establish an ongoing relationship with the organisation you have chosen to be the Benchmarking partner; once the channels of communication have been well and truly opened the process of exchanging information naturally becomes easier. Before your visit it should be agreed upon by both organisations exactly what material is to be exchanged, never asking for material from the partner that you would not also be willing to furnish them with.

The majority of Benchmarking activity will be governed by some form of mutual non-disclosure agreement. This means that the material you obtain from the partner must normally not be used for purposes other than those originally agreed. If you do wish to use the material, perhaps to give to a third party, do not use it without prior consent.

A structured professional approach to another organisation is imperative – it will help you get the best information from that organisation. If there is a mutual benefit for both parties, even better; it encourages organisations to be more open and more willing to exchange data.

Use the checklist in Figure 11. 1 or one of your own to optimise your visit.

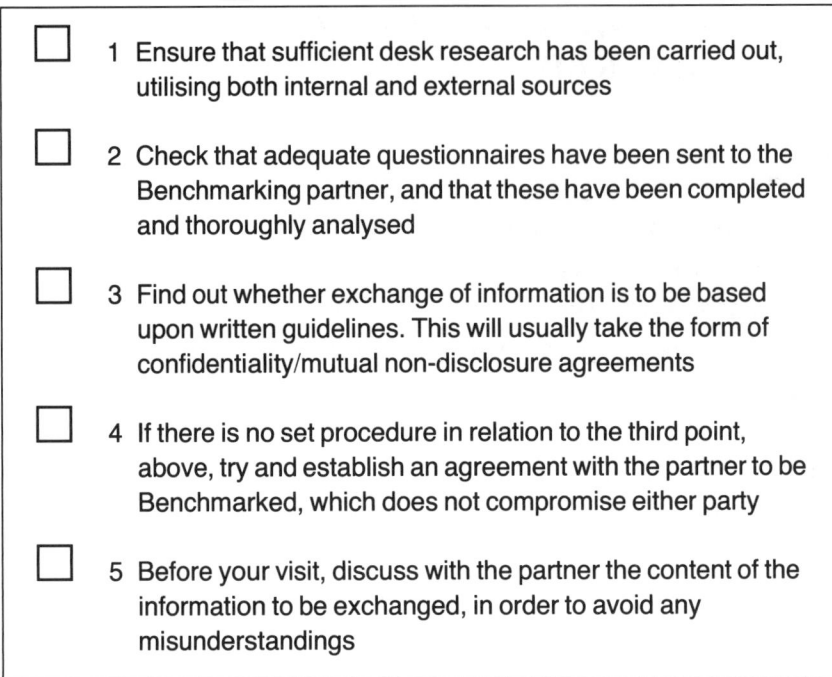

1 Ensure that sufficient desk research has been carried out, utilising both internal and external sources

2 Check that adequate questionnaires have been sent to the Benchmarking partner, and that these have been completed and thoroughly analysed

3 Find out whether exchange of information is to be based upon written guidelines. This will usually take the form of confidentiality/mutual non-disclosure agreements

4 If there is no set procedure in relation to the third point, above, try and establish an agreement with the partner to be Benchmarked, which does not compromise either party

5 Before your visit, discuss with the partner the content of the information to be exchanged, in order to avoid any misunderstandings

Figure 11.1   Optimising your visit to the partner to be Benchmarked

After the visit treat all contacts made through the Benchmarking activity with confidentiality. Obtain prior permission before reference is made either to the material obtained from the Benchmarking partner or to a third party when in an open forum.

In addition to all of this – take into consideration the legal aspects of Benchmarking. You can use the Benchmarking Code of Conduct, as put forward by the International Benchmarking Clearinghouse in the US, as a guide.

USE OF A DATABASE

Throughout the Benchmarking initiative, material will be researched, collated and stored. This should be put on to a database. Not only is this good practice, it also acts as a safety net by ensuring that the Benchmarking material is easily accessible, both to those members of the Benchmarking team, as well as those outside the team who may want to carry out a Benchmarking exercise of their own. The same ground will not be covered twice if there is a permanent record of all Benchmarking research and important time will not be wasted.

WHAT LEVEL TO BENCHMARK AT?

Those organisations which do have a significant market share by their very nature will have different requirements in relation to Benchmarking than the smaller organisation which might just be wanting to improve its Quality initiative. It therefore follows that the larger organisations will, out of necessity, search for those organisations who are 'best in the class', to maintain their place in the commercial market. In contrast, some smaller organisations can also benefit from the good practices of the larger, successful organisations in general.

ANALYSIS AND USE OF DATA

Once all information has been collected from the Benchmarking study there should be data which relate both to the current performance of the organisation and information which relates to those practices used by the partner who has been Benchmarked. The next stage is to compare the organisation's current performance with the performance of the chosen partner. The conclusion that an organisation may reach is that their own performance is actually superior in some of the areas Benchmarked – but there will still be lessons to be learnt. If you reach the conclusion that your performance is inferior, then there will be more major lessons. The organisation will be able to focus itself upon a set of criteria or quantified goals based upon the knowlege about its own performance and the performance of the organisation with which it Benchmarked.

IMPLEMENTATION

Once the decision is made to proceed, implementation of the changes must be planned and steered. New targets for the critical activity can be set based on the Benchmark data and good leadership will be essential to maintain focus and prevent backsliding. Progress towards the new objectives will need to be reviewed regularly, and senior management have a key role to play in overseeing and providing support for the whole implementation process.

THE ON-GOING INITIATIVE

The most successful organisations are aware that improvement is a never-ending journey. Benchmarking is part of this journey and can be seen as a tool successfully to change practices within an organisation. As such, it is an ongoing process and should be regularly reviewed – ensure that it is put on a regular agenda.

TROUBLESHOOTING BENCHMARKING ACTIVITY

Throughout your Benchmarking various problems may arise. Use Figure 11.2 as a guide for troubleshooting problems.

Problem	Likely causes	Solution
Benchmarking the wrong measure	Inadequate knowledge of own organisation and operations	Further research to find significant measure
Benchmarking the wrong organisation	Inadequate desk research	More detailed initial research
Benchmarking not leading to action	Senior management not involved	Ensure that management is seen to be in support
Failure to sell idea to senior management	Lack of information, poor presentation	Tie Best Practice Benchmarking firmly to the existing business plan; show how other companies have benefited
Lack of resources for Benchmarking	Lack of management support; exclusive ownership by the Best Practice Benchmarking team	Lobby and promote Best Practice Benchmarking as a company-wide approach
Data not meaningful	Too much/too little data; data not comparable	Tighter focus to measures; test the assumption about your processes that generated the measures
Inaccurate/false data	Over-reliance on public or competitor sources	Double-check sources through personal checks
Failure to sell idea to target organisations	Scepticism and protective instincts	Make clear the benefits of shared information; reassess criteria for selection of partners
Over-reliance on superficial similarity with partner	Lack of rigorous criteria for assessing partners	Redefine search to find closer fits
Benchmark partner unwilling to share useful data	Benchmark partner too alike	Define search by process not industry
Benchmark too many measures	Unclear priorities	Relate Best Practice Benchmarking to business plan

Source: 'Best Practice Benchmarking', DTI, 1992.

Figure 11.2   Troubleshooting

The Benchmarking Code of Conduct

- Keep it legal.
- Be willing to give what you get.
- Respect confidentiality.
- Keep information internal.
- Use benchmarking contacts.
- Don't refer without permission.
- Be prepared from the start.
- Understand expectations.
- Be honest.
- Following through with commitments.

Preamble

Benchmarking – the process of identifying and learning from best practices anywhere in the world is a powerful tool in the quest for continuous improvement.

To guide Benchmarking encounters and to advance the professionalisms and effectiveness of Benchmarking, the International Benchmarking Clearinghouse, a service of the American Productivity and Quality Center, and the Strategic Planning Institute Council on Benchmarking have adopted this common Code of Conduct. We encourage all organisations and individuals involved in Benchmarking to abide by this Code of Conduct. Adherence to these principles will contribute to efficient, effective, and ethical Benchmarking. This edition of the Code of Conduct has been expanded to provide greater guidance on the protocol of Benchmarking for beginners.

Individuals agree for themselves and their company to abide by the following principles for Benchmarking with other organisations.

1 Principle of <u>Legality</u>

1.1 If there is any potential question on the legality of an activity, don't do it.

1.2 Avoid discussions or actions that could lead to or imply an interest in restraint of trade, market and/or customer allocation schemes, price fixing, dealing arrangements, bid rigging, or bribery. Don't discuss costs with competitors if costs are an element of pricing.

1.3 Refraining from the acquisition of trade secrets from any means that could be interpreted as improper, including the breach or inducement of a breach of any duty to maintain secrecy. Do not disclose or use any trade secrets that may have been obtained through improper means or that was disclosed by another in violation of a duty to maintain its secrecy or limit its use.

1.4 Do not, as a consultant or client, extend one Benchmarking study's findings to another company without first obtaining the permission of the parties to the first study.

2 Principle of <u>Exchange</u>

2.1 Be willing to provide the same type and level of information that you request from your Benchmarking partner to your Benchmarking partner.
2.2 Communicate fully and early in the relationship to clarify expectations, avoid misunderstanding and establish mutual interest in the Benchmarking exchange.
2.3 Be honest and complete.

3 Principle of <u>Confidentiality</u>

3.1 Treat Benchmarking interchange as confidential to the individuals and companies involved. Information must not be communicated outside the partnering organisations without the prior consent of the Benchmarking pattern who shared the information.
3.2 A company's participation in a study is confidential and should not be communicated externally without their prior permission.

4 Principle of <u>Use</u>

4.1 Use information obtained through Benchmarking only for purposes of formulating improvement of operations or processes within the companies participating in the Benchmarking study.
4.2 The use or communication of a Benchmarking partner's name with the data obtained or practices observed requires the prior permission of that partner.
4.3 Do not use Benchmarking information or any information resulting from a Benchmarking exchange, or Benchmarking related networking as a means to market or sell.
4.4 Contact lists or other contact information provided by the International Benchmarking Clearinghouse in any form may not be used for marketing in any way.

5 Principle of <u>First Party Contact</u>

5.1 Initiate Benchmarking contacts whenever possible, through a Benchmarking contact designated by the partner company.
5.2 Respect the corporate culture of partner companies and work within mutually agreed procedures.
5.3 Obtain mutual agreement with the designated Benchmarking contact on any hand-off of communication or responsibility to other parties.

6 Principle of <u>Third Party Contact</u>

6.1 Obtain an individual's permission before providing his or her name in response to a contact request.

6.2 Avoid communicating a contact's name in an open forum without the contact's prior permission.

7 Principle of <u>Preparation</u>

7.1 Demonstrate commitment to the efficiency and effectiveness of Benchmarking by being prepared prior to making an initial Benchmarking contact.

7.2 Make the most of your Benchmarking partner's time by being fully prepared for each exchange.

7.3 Help your Benchmarking partners prepare by providing them with a questionnaire and agenda prior to Benchmarking visits.

8 Principle of <u>Completion</u>

8.1 Follow through with each commitment made to your Benchmarking partner in a timely manner.

8.2 Complete each Benchmarking study to the satisfaction of all Benchmarking partners as mutually agreed.

9 Principle of the <u>Understanding and Action</u>

9.1 Understand how your Benchmarking partner would like to be treated.

9.2 Treat your Benchmarking partner in the way that your Benchmarking partner would want to be treated.

9.3 Understand how your Benchmarking partner would like to have the information he or or she provides handled and used, and handle and use it in that manner.

BENCHMARKING PROTOCOL

Benchmarkers:

1 Know and abide by the Benchmarking Code of Conduct.

2 Have basic knowledge of Benchmarking and follow a Benchmarking process.

3 Prior to initiating contact with potential Benchmarking partners, have determined what to Benchmark, identified key performance variables to study, recognised superior performing companies and completed a rigorous self-assessment.

4 Have developed a questionnaire and interview guide, and will share these in advance if requested.

5 Possess the authority to share and be willing to share information with Benchmarking partners.

6 Work through a specified host and mutually agree on scheduling and meeting arrangements.

When the Benchmarking process proceeds to face-to-face site visit, the following behaviours are encouraged:

- Provide meeting agenda in advance
- Be professional, honest, courteous and prompt
- Introduce all attendees and explain why they are present
- Adhere to the agenda
- Use language that is universal, not one's own jargon
- Be sure that neither party is sharing proprietary information unless prior approval has been obtained by both parties, from the proper authority
- Share information about your own process and, if asked, consider sharing study results
- Offer to facilitate a future reciprocal visit
- Conclude meetings and visits on schedule
- Thank your Benchmarking partner for sharing their process

ETIQUETTE AND ETHICS

The following guidelines apply to both partners in a Benchmarking encounter with competitors or potential competitors:

- In Benchmarking with competitors, establish specific ground rules up-front, e.g. 'We don't want to talk about things that will give either of us a competitive advantage, but rather we want to see where we both can mutually improve or gain benefit.'
- Do not ask competitors for sensitive data or cause the Benchmarking partner to feel they must provide data to keep the process going.
- Use an ethical third party to assemble and 'blind' competitive data, with inputs from legal counsel in direct competitor sharing. (Note: When cost is closely linked to price, sharing cost data can be considered to be the same as price sharing.)
- Benchmarkers should check with legal counsel if any information gathering procedure is in doubt, e.g. before contacting a direct competitor. If uncomfortable, do not proceed, or sign a security/non-disclosure agreement. Instead, negotiate a specific non-disclosure agreement which will satisfy the attorney from both companies.
- Any information obtained from a Benchmarking partner should be treated as internal, privileged communication. If 'confidential' or proprietary material is to be exchanged, then a specific agreement should be executed to indicate the content of the material which needs to be protected, the duration of the period of protection, the conditions for permitting access to the material, and the specific handling requirements that are necessary for that material.

12 SUMMARY OF BENCHMARKING APPROACHES AND EXPERIENCES

INTRODUCTION

Learning from the first-hand experience of others is what Benchmarking is all about. This chapter briefly presents six organisations' experiences of Benchmarking, all written by employees of the individual organisations. These individuals have been directly involved with their organisations' Benchmarking initiative.

Their account of the organisations' approaches, and experiences of both internal and external Benchmarking follow.

COMPETITIVE BENCHMARKING AND ANALYSIS IN HEWLETT PACKARD, COMPUTER PERIPHERALS, BRISTOL

Introduction

Hewlett Packard's (HP) Bristol division manufactures most of HP's mass storage products for the European market, including disk, tape and optical storage devices. The division also has worldwide responsibility for the design and manufacture of Digital Audio Tape (DAT) computer backup tape drives, for which HP has approximately 50 per cent of the world market. We make both high performance drives for the Original

Equipment Manufacturer (OEM) market and Jetstore computer backup solutions (including software and hardware) which are sold via HP dealers.

At present the computer tape drive market is fiercely competitive with competition coming, not only from other DAT drive manufacturers, but also from other types of tape technology, and even from different technologies altogether.

Due to the intensity of the competition, competitive Benchmarking and analysis has become a priority within the division to help us tailor the division's activities to beat the competition. It has also become increasingly important to predict our competitors' future actions and competitive Benchmarking can give us information that allows this to be done with real data rather than 'gut feel'.

The main areas where Benchmarking contribute are as follows.

- Process Benchmarking. We use Industry and HP internal best practices to evaluate key divisional processes, such as manufacturing cycle times, order processing and financial performance.
- Product/service testing and Benchmarking. We buy competitor products and subject them to an intensive analysis, including strip-downs. We use this information in four main ways:
  - Tactical information for sales and marketing use;
  - Engineer education (R&D (research and development) and manufacturing);
  - Manufacturing cost estimates;
  - Strategic indications of competitor strengths, limitations and possible future directions.

Process Benchmarking

Process Benchmarking is used by each functional areas in the division. It is very useful because it provides information that helps ensure that we stay in-line or ahead of industry norms. It also provides targets for process improvement through TQM (Total Quality Management), which helps drive continuous process improvement in the division.

We find it relatively easy to find intra-company comparisons (with other divisions) and also comparisons with other companies who are not direct competitors. However, the really strategically important data would be R&D and manufacturing Benchmark data for companies with whom we compete directly. Unfortunately, this type of data is extremely difficult to obtain using legitimate methods and, for this reason, product Benchmarking has a higher focus in the division with resources specifically assigned to it.

Product Benchmarking

We believe that product Benchmarking can provide significant benefits over and above the obvious tactical 'know-your-competitor' marketing information and basic product analysis.

Far more useful, but unfortunately more difficult to achieve, is the type of strategic information that can help predict what type of products competitors will be producing, at what cost in the future.

We have found that it is possible to obtain this information by having a very focused programme to obtain public information concerning competitors (from industry analysts, press, patents, standards committees, customers and suppliers) along with strip-downs that aim to provide information on manufacturing cost, design limitations and future barriers, design strengths and future possibilities. When this information is collected and analysed over several product generations, it is possible to identify trends in the data such as:

- Current and future manufacturing cost comparisons;

- Product line growth limits (when will the competitor have to do revolutionary rather than evolutionary change?);
- Specific competitor time-to-market metrics;
- Competitor 'development mentality' – weaknesses and strengths, likely development paths.

This type of activity moves our Benchmarking activity to a more 'strategic' basis of competitive analysis that provides more information than the sum of each individual piece of information.

Summary

We believe that competitive Benchmarking provides us with an extremely effective way to improve the way we do business and also provides information which helps ensure that we remain in a leadership position for the long term.

As a first step, process and product Benchmarking can provide very useful data to drive processes improvements. However, to get more strategically useful information entails a much greater commitment of resources, and a more focused approach to information gathering and analysis over an extended period of time.

Steve Jerman *C. Eng MIEE*
Product Analyst
Product Marketing
Computer Peripherals Bristol

BENCHMARKING IN ICL

Benchmarking is a valuable method for improving a company's processes so as to increase the competitive advantage of their outputs. As with many other tools and techniques the initial problem is how and when to use Benchmarking in preference to other process improvement techniques. Within ICL this has taken time to identify but valuable lessons have been learnt on the way. Benchmarking is now a valuable tool in ICL's ongoing Quality and Business Improvement Programmes.

As part of ICL's quality programme the first internal guide on Benchmarking was produced in 1989. While generally accepted as a fine example of a Benchmarking technique, it was not readily taken up. This was partly because of the mystique surrounding the topic at the time and partly because of the more traditional, and well-known and well-used methods of improving output by competitive analysis and measurement of elements of the process. Consequently, over the last 18 months the position of Benchmarking against other process improvement techniques has been promoted, a recommended process has been established and facilitation has been provided. This has resulted in a specific and practical view of Benchmarking together with an appreciation of what is involved for the successful implementation of Benchmarking projects.

Benchmarking has been positioned against two other process improvement techniques and one output improvement method. The latter, Competitive Analysis, compares the outputs of the process against similar competitive outputs. It is usually undertaken by marketeers and results in new input requirements to the process. This, in turn, should produce revised or additional competitive advantage to the outputs of the process. The technique, often referred to as Competitive Benchmarking, does not generally affect the process itself.

For process improvement techniques, measurement of elements of the process can lead to process improvements and, in turn, enhance the attributes of the outputs. Measurement is relatively simple to undertake, can be done by owners and users of the process, and is not costly on resource. There are several techniques, ranging from Charting, Actual versus Theory Analysis, procedure validation and Six Sigma, all of which have their forte.

At the other extreme to measurement is Business Process Re-engineering. This is a technique which models, analyses and enacts the required process. This can lead to a completely new process with innovative and potentially completely different orientations of the output. It is costly, time-consuming and requires particular scarce expertise. In ICL we have positioned Benchmarking between Measurement and Business Process Re-engineering. As such, this offers process improvement for a balanced investment of time, resource and experience.

The Benchmarking process used in ICL is not mandatory. However, from the early production of an in-house 'Practice Guide to Benchmarking' produced in 1989, visits to several US companies recognised for their Benchmarking experience, particularly AT&T ('Benchmarking: Focus on World Class Practices'), the use of R. C. Camp's methodology (Benchmarking – The search for industry best practices that lead to superior performances, 1989) and Benchmarking projects, a preferred Benchmarking process has evolved. This has been communicated within the company through presentations and has been backed up by having experts to give overviews on Benchmarking practice, the do's and don'ts, the facilitation of the initial set-up of the project, and advise as and when requested. There is no central co-ordination of Benchmarking except for the establishment of a Registry of Benchmarks and the focused participation in the founding of the UK Benchmarking Centre.

The initiation of Benchmarks is numerous. However, ICL's prominence in quality initiative and practice, and the surveys the company undertakes with customers and the industry, provides many pointers as to where our processes may need improvement. In addition, we have made potential Benchmarking projects aware of the differing scope that Benchmarks can assume within the company, i.e. strategic, functional and operational. The former is mainly positioned at the corporate functions and relates to strategic planning, critical success factors and major business issues. The Benchmarks tend to be more complex to articulate than others and invariably could cause a fundamental change to the way in which the company operates. Functional Benchmarks are those involving processes that span a division or are part of the infrastructure of the company (e.g. finance, marketing). The associated processes are exceedingly important to the efficiency and effectiveness of the company, and, as such, the Benchmarks need particularly careful planning and executing. Operational Benchmarks tend to be those contained within a particular programme, project geography or group. The people undertaking the Benchmark are usually intimately involved, see the Benchmark as critical to the project or activity in hand and plan for a short timeframe to achieve results. The processes in these Benchmarks also tend to be easier to understand and, as such, are the oncs which are the types of Benchmark that are, recommended as a person's or group's first Benchmarking exercise.

ICL is involved in Benchmarking in three main ways, namely organisations who use ICL as Benchmark, Benchmarks initiated and undertaken by projects within ICL, and Benchmarks which involve consultancy groups as the prime drivers. While purists may argue that ICL being Benchmarked by other organisations cannot be classed as 'ICL Benchmarking', ICL gains significant information from both participating in the questioning and from the published results. Examples are an independent Benchmark on the process for producing Personal Computers, which has highlighted the strengths and weaknesses of our process, and a Benchmark by some of our OEM customers which has provided information into how ICL was positioned, and operated, as a vendor. While in this type of Benchmark a large element of the results are of the 'Competitive Analysis' type, significant information is produced which enables ICL to improve its processes.

In-house initiated Benchmarks have increased over the last two years. This has been brought about by the increased understanding of the subject, its positioning and, above all, the need to improve our business competitiveness. Some Benchmarks have been revisited either to widen their scope (e.g. investment management) or to narrow their scope (e.g. integration information availability). This is not to imply that the original Benchmarking project was not valid but more to recognise the importance of the process to the business and the potential for further improvements that Benchmarking can bring. Results in these areas have shown that ICL is well positioned against best practice. A particularly large Benchmark has been undertaken against the processes which form part of ICL's overall customer care activity. Several processes, encompassing survey formulation and measurement criteria, have been Benchmarked both internally and externally. The resulting information has been instrumental in not only enhancing the processes themselves, but also providing new ideas for the overall Customer Care activity. Two current Benchmarks which have recently been initiated relate to support processes which are aimed at customer satisfaction and the processes involved in producing a Service, as opposed to a product, for the market place.

Benchmarking with the help of consultancy companies has both its advantages and disadvantages. Generally, the Benchmark can command a wider range of resources and topic knowledge, and can achieve economies of scale when the Benchmark is done with like-minded groups of companies. Against this, one has to accept the compromises of the whole group as to the processes to be Benchmarked. ICL has been involved in several Benchmarks over the last two years using consultancies, notably systems architecture formulation, supply chain management and electronic systems assembly. In 1993, ICL is also the main sponsor of a Logistics Benchmark and joint sponsor for Benchmarking the Project Management process.

From all the Benchmarking activities that have been undertaken many lessons have been learnt: some of technique, some do's and some don'ts. Five that always need to be emphasised before and during a Benchmarking project are as follows:

- Gain management commitment and sponsorship to the Benchmarking project – this will be needed to sustain the project and implement the resulting actions.
- Take time to select the process to be Benchmarked and thoroughly understand the process before selecting Benchmarking partners – failure in this area will produce a poor return for the Benchmarking project.
- Selecting Benchmarking partners is difficult – set criteria for selecting a process within another company – it's the process you are selecting, not the company itself
- The Benchmarking project will require expertise and time – results will not be obtained in a short time (cf. competitive analysis which gives a relatively quick comparison of output, which can then be input as requirements to the process).
- Be prepared for results from the Benchmark which may not always be what you expected – the process you have may be so poor that you may need to consider re-engineering or abandoning the process, either because it does not adequately support the strategy of the company or because the investment to improve the process may be too great.

Overall, Benchmarking is a tool in an armoury of methods and techniques that can help improve processes to gain greater competitive advantage of the outputs. Used in the correct way Benchmarking does engender business improvement.

David G. Smith
Manager, Operations
OPENframework Division
ICL

THE ROVER GROUP APPROACH

Benchmarking at Rover is seen as an important tool supporting the change necessary for the group to be successful in the late 1990s. It does not stand alone and is linked to our philosophy that every individual's contribution is vital, that everyone has two tasks, namely their work and the improvement of that work, and that the mutual commitment of everyone in and supporting the company through teamwork, will give competitive advantage.

The first steps in developing this philosophy began to be put in place in 1987, when the company embarked on a Total Quality Training Initiative for all its 33,000 employees. Four key issues, of relevance to Benchmarking, came out of this training:

1 Acceptance of the Customer as Driver of your process (both internal and external);
2 Acceptance that all could contribute and that learning, even by mistakes, was important;
3 Acceptance that measurement at every level is vital;
4 Providing the tools of analysis and problem solving to all.

A key to achieving such competitive advantage is a willingness to learn, a preparedness to copy and an ability to achieve process alignment to meet company goals. Benchmarking was seen as a means to help achieve this at two levels, strategic and operational.

It has been developed at Rover unashamedly in copying what others had done in this field, particularly Rank Xerox. The process we use is essentially simple as shown in Figure 12.2.

At the strategic level Rover has identified target areas for Benchmarking by identifying four strategic thrusts along the direction in which we considered we needed to move to ensure the success of the business: four factors critical for our success.

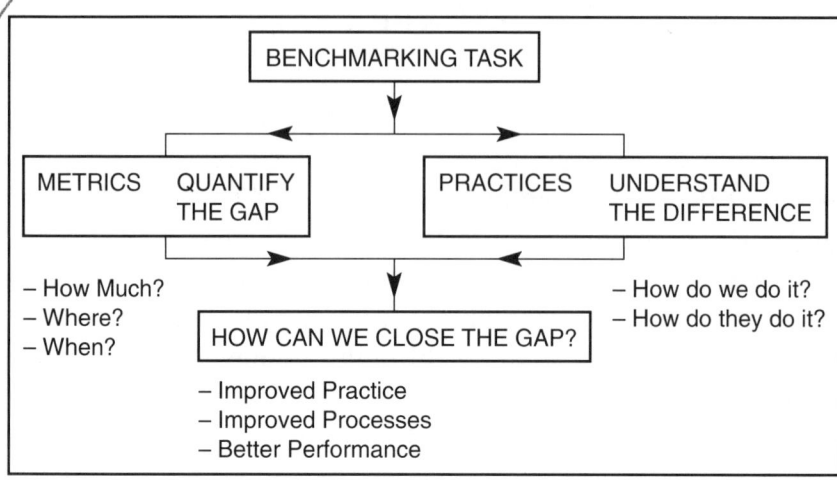

Figure 12.1   Benchmarking at Rover

Rover at the same time analysed its business and developed a macro model of seven key operational processes. We then developed a matrix of the key characteristics within these processes which we considered should be in place as the consequence of successfully accomplishing our four strategic thrusts.

Macro performance metrics were developed for these characteristics mainly by desk-top research, but where data were not available or contradictory, by company visits to both competitors and non-competitors. These macro measures were used to assist the company in prioritising processes needing maximum attention.

Significant benefit was achieved merely by using the total quality analysis books to examine our current process in these areas and to start, step by step, to close the competitive gap. Absolute accuracy of the metrics obtained this way was not vital, for if a significant gap was indicated, it alone provided stimulus for improvement.

At operational level it was vital in order for Benchmarking to succeed that commitment and clarity of strategic direction were obvious and clearly defined from the top. Each business unit in Rover therefore developed four to eight critical success factors

(CSFs) related to the company's four strategic thrusts, but specifically aligned to that business's need. The processes related to those CSFs were defined and the critical performance measures developed. Most of these, unlike previous measures, of control being non-financial, e.g. delivery lead time, cycle time achievement etc. This process of determining CSFs for critical processes, prioritising and developing measures is being pursued throughout the company. Benchmarking in the full sense of total process comparison taking place at as low a level as possible in the organisation. It is Rover's view that for full Benchmarking to be effective, factholders who are the ones who will implement any results should also be the ones who carry out the Benchmarking. This ensures full understanding and ownership of processes and their improvement.

Of key importance for the success of Benchmarking is the ability to learn from example within the company. To do this Rover have developed several forums for the interchange of information within the company as part of the Rover learning process. With full Benchmarking being an expensive operation in terms of human resource, such a process is important if maximum benefit is to be achieved.

To date Rover have found Benchmarking to be useful as one of the many levers of change required to ensure a successful future for the company

Mike James-Moore
Manager, Manufacturing Strategy
Rover Group

BENCHMARKING AT BOC SPECIAL GASES

In BOC Special Gases Benchmarking is a technique that has been used for a number of years. Because of the highly specialised nature of our business and a relatively small number of players worldwide Benchmarking exercises have tended to be inter-company, inter-business or non-commercial non-sensitive areas such as safety.

Inter-company

Benchmarking of similar operations within a group of companies can yield some very interesting trends and highlight differences. One problem that has to be overcome when Benchmarking on an international scale is the effect of currency movements and widely differing interest rates and Retail Price Index movements. With thought in structuring the questionnaire these can easily be overcome.

Areas which BOC Special Gases Benchmarks with nine other similar companies worldwide include:

- Sales growth revenue and volume;
- Profit growth;
- Return on assets;
- Plant utilisation;
- Sales growth broken down into markets;
- Technology best practices.

From our experience the value in Benchmarking comes from the dialogue that the process stimulates. For example the table below shows asset utilisation over a three-year period for five of our operations.

Company	A %	B %	C %	D %	E %
Year 1	70.9	84.8	71.4	84.8	57.7
Year 2	69.5	83.7	72.5	69.0	59.0
Year 3	71.0	N/A	72.0	70.0	60.5

A benchmarking exercise such as this raises a raft of questions – Company B appears to be the odd man out in that he drives his assets very hard while Company E is clearly different at the other end of the scale. In isolation these data are useless and as a consequence we use the data mainly to stimulate discussion between the companies in order to find the issues that create the differences.

Customer satisfaction

A major use of Benchmarking for Special Gases is in the area of customer satisfaction. For a number of years we have been conducting research aimed at highlighting our weaknesses opposite our competition. The market research is carried out by an external consultant using both face-to-face and telephone interviews. It is our policy always to declare that commencement of the interview that it is being carried out on behalf of BOC.

Questions are focused around two quality issues, the quality of our service and the quality of our products.

A typical question would be 'On a score of 1 to 10 with 1 being low how would you rate BOC's speed of delivery?' This question would then be revisited in two other ways later in the questionnaire. 'On the same score how do you rate BOC's delivery reliability?' The questions are then repeated, but this time asking the customer to rank us against our competition. In this way we have an absolute view of our performance by our customers and a comparative view.

Based upon this extremely valuable Benchmarking work we have been able to bring about radical change in our business. For example, some years ago a survey of 10 per cent of our largest market segment gave us some clear data which told us that our delivery performance was weak in absolute terms and was falling back against a small competitor. We felt that the data were so significant that we established a task force to find a solution. After six months of intense study of the problem with multi-discipline teams we eventually decided to use JIT (just in time) to provide the main plank of the solution.

This is a clear example where data from a Benchmarking exercise were used to accomplish a fundamental change in the way in which a part of our business was run.

Steve Waldron
General Manager
BOC Ltd

BENCHMARKING AT IBM

BM and Benchmarking have been together for a long time – since the early days of computers when performance comparisons were conducted against competitors' products and product MIPS rates (Millions of Instructions per second) determined.

There are two watersheds in the IBM history of Benchmarking. The first occurred in the late 1970s with the publication of a corporate instruction that required that all new products (both hardware and software) must have superior performance to both their IBM precursor and the best of the competitions' products, from the time of first customer shipment. The result of this was that product Benchmarking became firmly established throughout the corporation. It became a matter of routine for all IBM products to be Benchmarked against the competition (successfully demonstrating superior performance is a condition of product announcement) – Benchmarked in terms of function, reliability and availability. The sources of data are:

- Specially commissioned customer surveys;
- Standard industry surveys such as 'Reliability Plus';
- Laboratory testing of competitors' products.

The second watershed was the establishment of the Malcolm

Baldrige National Quality award in the US, and its subsequent adoption as the corporate assessment methodology by IBM. Baldrige places heavy emphasis on continuous improvement, with all processes expected to have feedback loops built into them and to be compared with industry best practice. This has resulted in the IBM Benchmarking activity being expanded to cover all its processes as well as its products.

Early activity was focused on establishing the pre-conditions for process Benchmarking:

- Provision of training for all involved personnel;
- Basic process management – (identifying which processes are the priorities for Benchmarking, assign process owners, perform process mapping, implementing process measurements).

Process Benchmarking itself did not start until all these activities were completed. In a multinational Corporation like IBM there is a very real danger of several individuals in separate locations around the world starting independent Benchmarking activities of the same business process. To control this a corporate database was established. All Benchmark reports are filed in it so that the results can be shared among all interested parties.

The following example illustrates the use of Benchmarking in IBM and the benefits that have resulted from it. Figure 12.2 shows some of the Benchmarking activities under way at the Manufacturing and Development Division in Havant. As can be seen, the Benchmarking activity covers the spectrum from the product and production processes through to customer satisfaction and internal business processes.

The example chosen is the manufacturing process for Communication Controllers. The first step in this exercise was to understand Havant's manufacturing process. The factors that were important for the process to achieve its objectives were established and a scoring methodology devised. The process

Business area	Comparison sources	Criteria used	Uses of data
1) Product quality			
Flex	Roome, Teac Toshiba	Customer needs/direction	Process improvement, production design, Strategy development
Network, systems	GEC, Ferranti, Fortronic, McDonnell Douglas, IBM Santa Palomba	Business Perf, Product and process leadership	Process improvement, shorten lead times to make engineering challenge and introduce new products
Storage production	Hitachi, Western Digital, Seagate, Siemens, Minscribe Rodime, Praritech, Connor Fujitsu, Quantum	Product cost/ performance, technology projections	Product design and quality, process improvement
Subsystems	Press, consultants, databases, exhibitions int/ext contacts	Product price/ performance, feature mix	Product design – ensuring product is BOB
2) Customer satisfaction			
Customer satisfaction	To be determined	Key site needs	Improve understanding of current and future needs
3) Internal operations			
New product introduction	To be determined	Cycle time, key site process	Shorten cycle time from design to max throughput, reduce cycle time
Product cost management	To be determined	Key site process	
New business opportunities	To be determined	Key site process, skills, cycle time, revenue	Define BOB process
Education	Westlands	BOB process	Improve methods
EC management	Internal (design practices)	Cycle time BOB	Reduce cycle times
Facilities request	Internal (EMEA MFG)	BOB Process	Process improvement
4) Supplier performance			
Supply/demand	To be determined	BOB supply organisations	Reduce variability and improve responsiveness

Figure 12.2   Summary of IBM Competitiveness Analysis and Benchmarking activity

Manufacturing process parameter Score 20 = Best v. Target 0 = Worst v. Target	Competitive manufacturing Benchmark									
	Base score	IBM HVT	A	B	C	D	E	F	IBM Pos	B Co
New line set up										
Minimum ECs	20	10	19	10	10	10	12	12	4	19
Minimum capital equipment	20	15	20	15	13	16	14	13	3	20
Minimum test code/prog change	20	12	20	12	12	12	4	6	2	20
Minimum time IBP to build	20	8	19	8	8	8	10	10	4	19
Minimum Operator Training	20	14	20	14	14	14	8	12	2	20
Category Total	100	59	98	59	57	60	48	53	3	98
Build process										
Minimum part numbers	20	12	20	10	10	11	14	12	3	20
Minimum stock levels	20	16	5	10	10	18	14	18	3	18
Minimum time file	20	15	20	17	16	14	12	16	5	20
Minimum order to ship time	20	10	20	10	7	15	6	13	4	20
Minimum number of vendors	20	15	15	18	12	13	15	16	3	18
Category Total	100	68	80	65	55	71	61	75	4	90
Quality & reliability										
Minimum field defects	20	16	20	12	18	18	19	13	5	20
Minimum goods-in defects	20	17	18	15	18	18	19	16	5	19
Minimum test defects	20	15	16	15	15	14	18	14	3	18
Minimum Line defects	20	16	17	14	13	12	18	14	3	18
Minimum time in test	20	14	19	12	16	12	10	15	4	19
Category Total	100	78	90	68	80	74	84	72	4	94
Management process										
Minimum paper control system	20	17	20	12	17	18	18	14	4	20
Minimum ME/TE/PE staff	20	14	18	12	14	14	10	16	3	15
Minimum Mat'ls supply staff	20	15	10	15	14	17	10	16	3	17
Minimum order process	20	14	18	14	14	16	10	16	4	18
Minimum Mat'ls handling staff	20	15	10	10	13	17	14	16	3	17
Category Total	100	75	76	63	72	82	62	78	4	90
Customer satisfaction										
Best quality	20	18	18	15	18	14	18	16	1	18
Delivery on time	20	15	19	14	13	16	12	16	4	19
Most options/features	20	14	18	16	16	14	14	16	5	18
Best response to order churn	20	15	10	13	15	18	10	18	3	18
Best price/discounts	20	12	14	12	12	12	15	14	4	15
Category Total	100	74	79	70	74	74	69	80	3	88
Overall Benchmark Total	500	354	423	325	338	361	324	358	4	466

Figure 12.3   IBM communication controller – comparative scoring

was scored, on a scale of 0–20, for each of the parameters that had been defined (see Figure 12.3).

This gave a baseline – how the current process performed in comparison to the ideal. The next stage was to compare it to the best to be found among other UK manufacturers that operated similar processes. In fact, one of the sites visited was that of a canned food manufacturer. Although this manufacturer scored highly on most of the parameters (and was the overall 'winner'), the processes operated were so dissimilar that the approaches used couldn't be adapted to the IBM manufacturing line.

IBM then focused on those manufacturers that were involved in the electronics industry. Some were direct competitors in the communication controller market, others manufactured products that had similar process requirements but were in market areas in which IBM does not operate. Identification of these manufacturers as potential best practice sites was done by a mix of literature research and DTI publications. Each of the sites was visited by a team from Havant that contained skills in manufacturing engineering, test engineering, process design and competitive analysis. After each visit, the team scored the site on each of the parameters. When this had been done, a gap analysis was conducted. IBM was compared to the 'best of breed' for each of the parameters, the reason for the superior performance understood, and plans developed as to how the parameter could be adopted, improved and implemented in Havant.

The result was the identification of 22 implementable improvements that reduced cost, improved product lead times, improved product quality or generally resulted in engineering improvements.

Barrie Povey
Quality Consultant
IBM

BENCHMARKING AT ABBEY NATIONAL

Background

Have you ever sat through a series of conference presentations wondering just what idea you are going to go way with?

I was at such a conference about a year and half ago, and the one idea I came away with related to clarity of information. It was a question of 'How do you present a single index of customer satisfaction in relation to a multi-disciplined organisation with a range of products?'

I saw one simple slide as part of an overall package that crystallised the concept for me and it looked like this (see Figure 12.4). This gives a clear indication of satisfaction with an area of operation. Then, following on from that was a concluding slide which showed the answer to the most fundamental of questions: 'As a result of this transaction will you remain loyal with our organisation?' (see Figure 12.5).

Customer satisfaction

This was only the germ of an idea – I had only picked up one small aspect of customer satisfaction but I wanted to develop it further. I didn't want to have to reinvent the wheel, however, so I took the bull by the horns and went to the presenter, and asked if I could learn more about what was behind the scenes. And so I was introduced to Royal Mail, who operated a most comprehensive study into customer satisfaction. My local regional manager lost no time in inviting me to have a look round his operation and see in detail not only his customer satisfaction measuring process, but also the fruits of such an exercise.

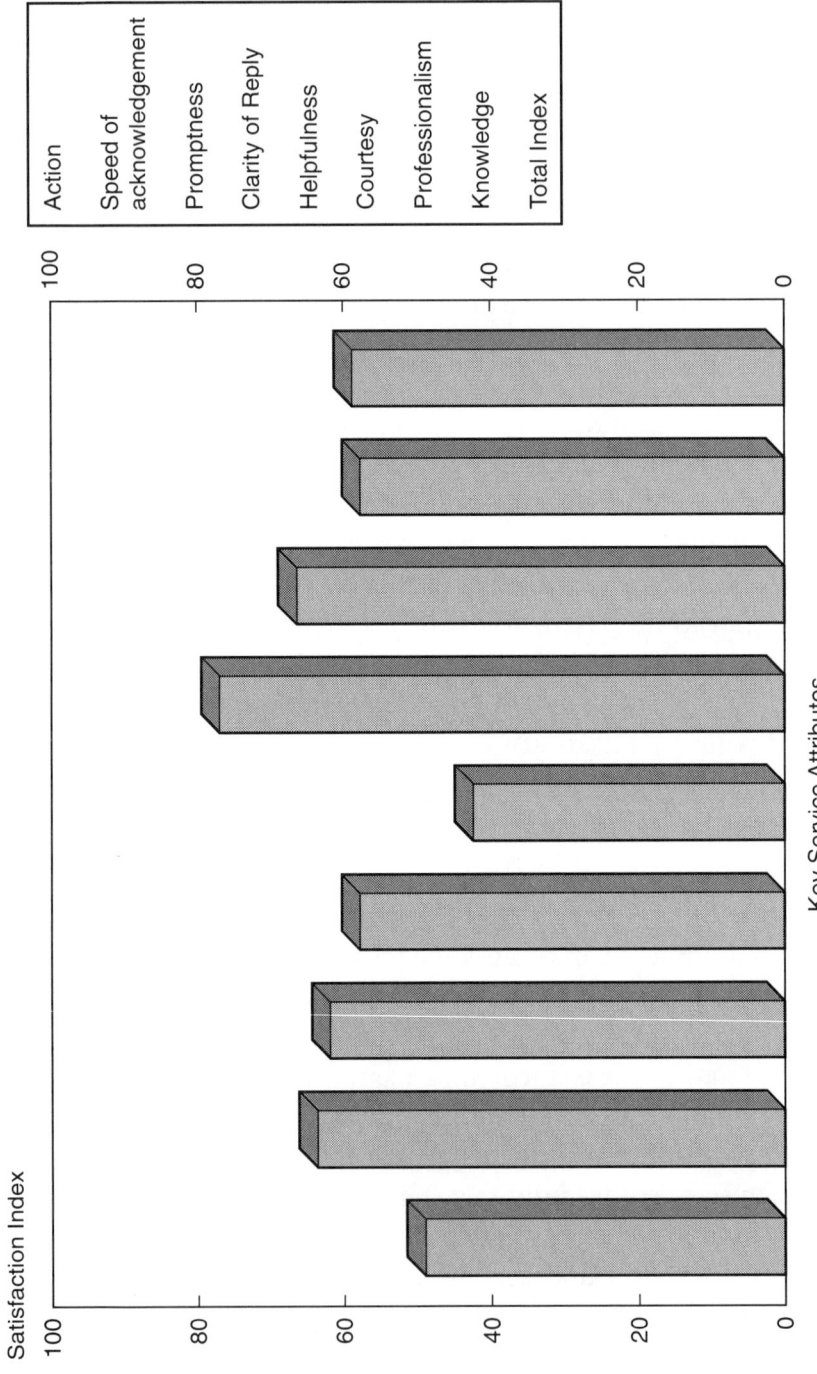

Figure 12.4   Customer satisfaction index

Due to our handling of the matter, will you remain a customer?

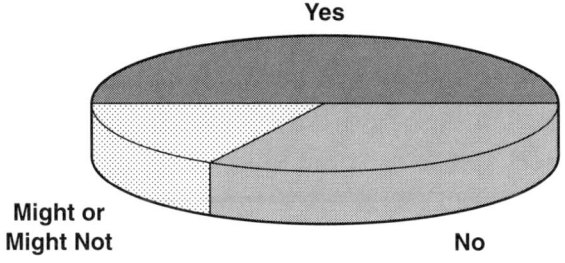

Figure 12.5   Customer satisfaction index: customer retention

Not content with giving me the bare bones and allowing me to go away and reinvent the wheel, I was taken through the exercise in detail and even introduced to the independent agency that selected the random sample, processed the data and finally presented the information in a format appropriate for Senior Management.

The first steps

I realised that Royal Mail's scheme was company wide and it would have been over-ambitious of me to consider introducing something on that scale straight away. But with advice and guidance I decided to introduce a pilot scheme within my own department, Group Customer Relations.

One of the first steps I took was to discover what exactly was important to my customers. It was all very well considering an exercise aimed at measuring satisfaction in the postal market, but what about customers complaining to the centre of a large financial institution? I took some advice and simply went out and asked the customers two questions. First, in terms of customer service 'what was important *to them*'. Second, what had made them satisfied about the process that we had just put them through. Building on experience that had been shared with me, I investigated further and asked customers what the main issues were surrounding their complaints. I asked them to rank and weight these according to their concerns. We then sent a questionnaire to a 50 per cent sample of our customers asking them to rate our performance against seven key criteria. I thought it would be a nice idea to say to these customers that if they still had a concern perhaps they would like to tell me about it. They had so much to say, I'm still reading their answers!

Customer response

The response was amazing. As the Royal Mail had told me, 'Carefully word your questionnaire and you will get over 50 per cent response'. We reached 65 per cent. The exercise provided us with useful information, not only of how we handled the complaint, but also on how we might avoid the problem in the future.

At present, I have over six months of data. I now feel I am in a position seriously to consider recommending that we extend the application of such a customer satisfaction index across the company.

At the same time as this exercise was taking place I was approached by another organisation asking me to share with them some of the experience we had gained in satisfying customers. An international courier company, they had just conducted a survey among some of their clients to determine who were the best in terms of providing excellent customer service. Abbey National was among those acknowledged to provide a high standard of service. Naturally the courier company were eager to find out why this might be. They were particularly interested in the way in which we managed the customer complaints process I invited them in to see our operation and shared with them what information I could. As part of their reciprocal arrangement, I recently went to see how they managed their customer service area.

Key performance indicators

One of the main aspects of their business was the provision of key performance indicators (KPIs). These are just half a dozen statistics that really serve to focus the minds of Senior Management on a particular area of operation.

Making use of this and the earlier lesson gained from Royal Mail I now regularly produce a brief but comprehensive summary of my Department's customer service standards along the following lines:

- Summary and trends of the five most frequent issues;
- Complaint analysis by product, service category, source and cause;
- Customer satisfaction by key performance criteria;
- Customer loyalty statement and trend.

Conclusion

Life is all about learning – learning from one another. And in business, it is no different. I've found some people who are only too willing to share information in the firm belief that we have all got something that we can improve upon. When we get together and share information these days, it's called Benchmarking, and I can recommend it.

What's next?

The European Foundation for Quality Management (EFQM) is trying hard to spread awareness of its TQM model. As part of their initiative, they are encouraging networking and Benchmarking across the whole community, and that can only enhance the position of Western European business in the world market.

John Smith
Group Customer Relations Manager
Abbey National PLC

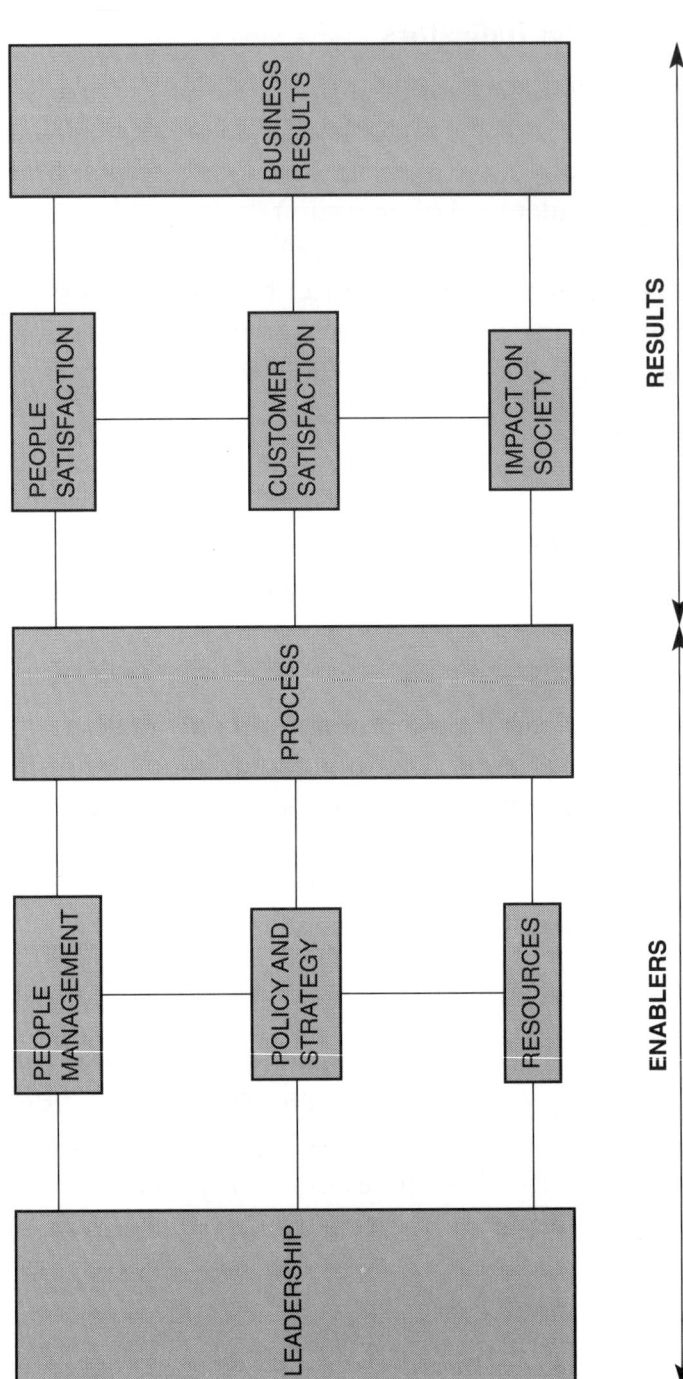

Figure 12.6   EQFM model

BENCHMARKING IN BRITISH GAS

Introduction

In November 1992, the new Managing Director for the UK Gas Business commissioned a research project on Benchmarking. Contact with other organisations had led to the conviction that Benchmarking could represent a key instrument in driving performance improvement and culture change. A project team of four was formed for three months with the objective of answering the following questions.

- What is Benchmarking?
- What different varieties exist?
- How have other companies and consultancies used Benchmarking?
- What were the key lessons they learnt/what is Benchmarking best practice?
- How should Benchmarking be used in UK Gas Business?

How does British gas see Benchmarking?

As one author recently pointed out, there is no single definition of Benchmarking – select from a set of key phrases the characteristics you want to emphasise and you have your own definition. The British Gas definition goes as follows:

> Benchmarking is the continuous process of identifying, comparing and learning from world class best products, services and practices to set the agenda for change and promote a culture of continuous improvement within an organisation.

The shorthand version which has subsequently been emphasised in briefing senior management is 'a planned and structured method of learning from outside the Company'. The emphasis is on 'planned and structured'.

What different varieties exist?

It soon became clear that a wide spectrum of approaches to Benchmarking existed. The team labelled the outer limits of the spectrum as the 'Management Accountant' approach and the 'TQ' approach.

- The Management Accountant approach, at its 'worst', is typified by a concern with cost or manpower numbers alone. Once a company is found whose 'metrics'/efficiency ratios are better, the internal targets can be reset and management driven to achieve the new targets. The poor management victims are unlikely to believe the figures and certainly will not know how the competitors are achieving better performance. Success rate, consequently, is unlikely to be high.

- The TQ approach at its worst can be concerned only with detailed processes. It has the merit that it normally involves 'grass roots' staff, but the processes may not be critical to business success. The greatest danger is that the process improvement project has no clear objective other than 'improvement'. Is the objective a 20 per cent reduction in cost or a 30 per cent improvement in service quality or is it just to make people feel better? Again success can be limited.

In a more conventional sense, the varieties of Benchmarking and the levels at which it could be employed are expressed in Figure 12.8 which points to the fact that generic Benchmarking at the strategic and business management level can have the greatest effect on a company's performance.

How have other companies and consultancies used Benchmarking?

What was initially surprising was the number of major companies in the UK which had used Benchmarking for some time and the massive level of interest in it. Less surprising was its use

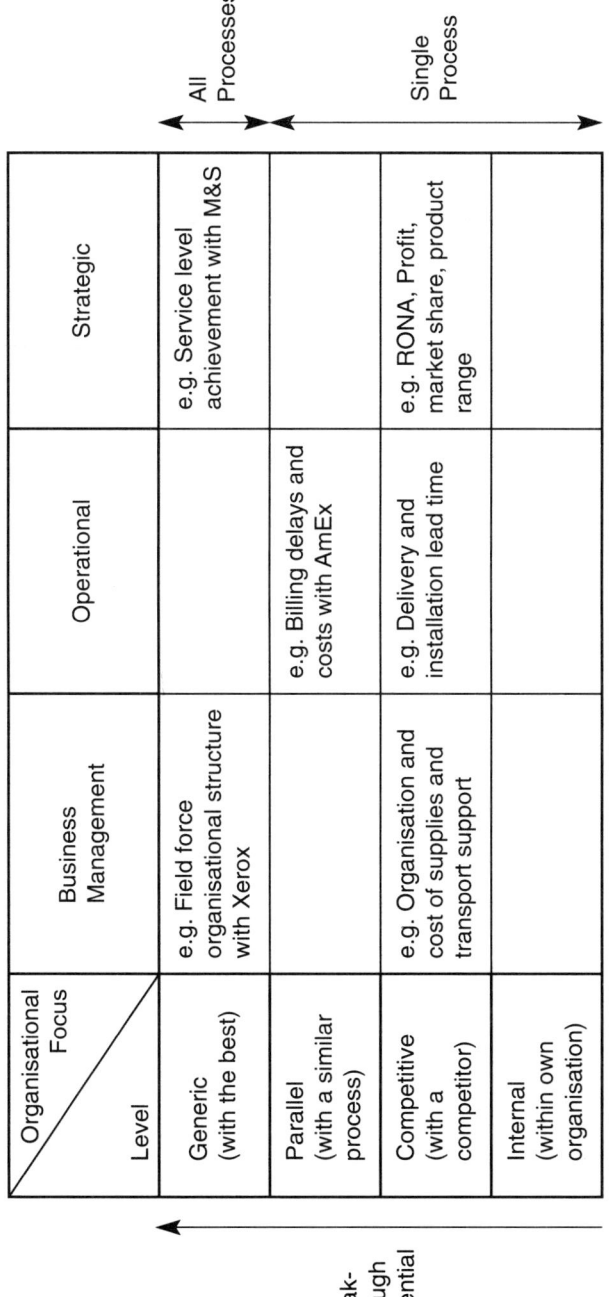

Figure 12.7

in the US where it 'originated'. In particular, the utilities in the US, driven by ever watchful regulators, were extensive users of Benchmarking – efficiency ratios of every variety abounded.

Equally, Benchmarking has been used to address every facet of management, from innovation and quality through product design and process improvement to cost reduction and efficiency improvement.

What also became clear was that the companies which had most successfully used Benchmarking were generally faced with an urgent business need, driven either by a real threat to business survival or an often externally imposed need to effect radical changes.

What were the key lessons they learnt/what is Benchmarking best practice?

Interviews conducted with over 25 companies currently using Benchmarking focused clearly on identifying the key lessons which had been learnt. These are recorded below:

Benchmarking should:

- Recognise the effort needed to establish like-for-like efficiency metrics;
- Be driven by business needs;
- Be based on an understanding of the processes and Critical Success Factors;
- Be based on trends;
- Be planned in detail;
- Be conducted by managers themselves;
- Be led by a 'champion';
- Use a range of qualitative and quantitative measures;
- be adopted as a TQ tool.

Benchmarking should not:

- Be used simply to reset targets, i.e. using metrics as a stick;

- Be delegated to consultants;

- Be used to justify the status quo, e.g. to a regulator.

Benchmarking is:

- Time consuming to do thoroughly;

- Valuable if under threat or undergoing major change.

How should Benchmarking be used in British Gas?

Benchmarking, as the books rightly say, should address real business needs. At the time the UK Gas Business was placing considerable emphasis on a cost reduction programme.

One solution then would be to identify highest priority, highest cost areas of the business and the processes within them, and seek out 'champions' in those areas to head Benchmarking initiatives.

However, the Company was at the time embarking on a review of strategy in its five major markets.

- Transportation;
- Contract Gas Supply;
- Public Gas Supply;
- Appliance Retailing;
- Installation and Contracting/Customer Service.

This would require a major rethink of strategic objectives and plans in each market area. So the concept emerged that Benchmarking should be employed to support this development work. The simple model may be seen in Figure 12.8.

Proposals to employ Benchmarking as a key instrument in the reappraisal of strategy were accepted. Five project teams, one for each market, were formed with senior leadership. Benchmarking would be used to provide the external perspective necessary to position UK Gas Business in the markets which would evolve in the mid to late 1990s.

Figure 12.8

A simple example here will illustrate the way in which Benchmarking would be used. A Benchmarking exercise in the appliance retailing area looking at white goods retailers both in the UK and abroad could assist in shaping:

- Showroom strategy (how many, where, what image);
- Product strategy (what type, what range);
- National organisation (best practice, marketing and sales management structures);
- Manning levels and payment systems;
- Profitability targets.

At the time of writing, the teams have been formed and their training in Benchmarking has commenced. The commitment to injecting the external perspective via Benchmarking is solid.

The use of generic Benchmarking at the strategic and business management level was only one strand of the proposals on Benchmarking. By this route, 25–30 people would gain an external perspective and experience of the technique. One of the objectives, however, was culture change – hence the agreement to employ external Benchmarking within the already active Total Quality Strategy in the Company. Management and staff at all levels would be encouraged to use Benchmarking and be briefed on it. Quality improvement teams would receive training in Benchmarking using materials developed jointly with Xerox Quality Solutions – this would supplement existing techniques training for Quality Improvement teams.

These two initiatives are now launched. The next year will provide British Gas with a significant experience of Benchmarking at two very different levels of the organisation. That experience will undoubtedly determine the future deployment of Benchmarking in the Company.

Ian D.B. Ferguson
Head of Personnel Resources
British Gas PLC

13 THE FUTURE OF BENCHMARKING

Will the 'Benchmarking Boom' go away? It is hard to think so. Benchmarking, after all, is something that we should have been doing, to some extent what we have been doing, for years. Organisations are slow to change, but increasingly there is a recognition that the old functional structures with little cross-functional activity are increasingly out of date, and the question is more how to implement Benchmarking and how to make it a routine part of organisational life.

In broad terms, those who have started will not stop. The Benchmarking Clearinghouse survey revealed that 96 per cent of the firms in the US sample of Benchmarkers expect more or significantly more Benchmarking in the next five years. Indeed, 75 per cent of those organisations reported an increase in Benchmarking in the last year, two thirds of them have already been Benchmarked by another US company and two-thirds report that Benchmarking is in use at least at some of their US-based competitors. Sixty-eight per cent of the UK CBI study also indicated plans to increase Benchmarking in the next five years.

It is this increase in commercial awareness that lies at the heart of the Benchmarking Boom. The competitive pressure to improve the quality of products, service and management effectiveness is clearly a major factor in causing organisations to look for better practice elsewhere. Levels of competition within the US market place and overseas, and perceptions of this competition, have increased greatly over the last five years, and, clearly, the same is true in the UK and Europe.

However good Benchmarking is, Blanket Benchmarking is not a sensible proposition. Only 6 per cent of the US study indicated that they were going to try and Benchmark all processes, and only 13 per cent that they were going to try and Benchmark all competitors. The selection of Benchmarking partners and processes to Benchmark needs to be done very carefully.

Like all new methods appearing on the business scene, Benchmarking is not being applied consistently perfectly. Companies clearly have to learn how to do it, when they should do it and what to avoid. Like most new management concepts, there is evidence of inadequate planning. The US study reported that 84 per cent of companies surveyed reported that their firms do not yet have a strategic Benchmarking plan. This is worrying, since unsuccessful Benchmarking is frequently the result of poor planning.

Management support is also not always what it should be, despite the fact that in the US survey 90 per cent of the companies engaged in Benchmarking had an active Total Quality Management programme. Management education is essential and training is necessary at all levels, particulary for Benchmarking teams. Most organisations (83 per cent) consider themselves to be beginners or novices at Benchmarking. While 51 per cent of the US companies surveyed believe that it will not be difficult to sustain enthusiasm for Benchmarking over the next five years, 30 per cent are not sure if the current excitement about Benchmarking will be maintained and 19 per cent say it will be difficult.

The sharing of Benchmarking information is a natural part of the Benchmarking process, and does have a major impact on the cost-effectiveness of the approach and the ease of targeting results. Such sharing is facilitated if information can be kept anonymous or mutual benefit deals are possible. There is a need for infrastructures to be developed to assist this and, clearly, the UK needs its equivalent of the American International

Benchmarking Clearinghouse. Such a centre could also take a European role. Quite possibly, small organisations will need special support to help them conduct Benchmarking studies given their limited resources and special support is likely to be needed also in the difficult areas for Benchmarking, like the creative service sector.

Finally, as well as a strategy for Benchmarking – at the company and at the national level – there is also a need for the Benchmarking of strategy. It is not just a question of business processes, physical product and functional areas; it is also a question of how you are going to enter, influence and develop the market; plan, organise and run your manufacturing or service delivery operation; how you are going to manage your portfolio of interests; how you are going to structure your development organisation; how you are going to survive and grow in the future. We end where we began. Benchmarking is about doing the obvious things in a systematic manner. Consultants cannot 'solve it all'; they can help, but you must own it.

14 ASSESSING YOUR STARTING POINT AND BUILDING AN ACTION PLAN

Having read this book, you will now appreciate the importance of Benchmarking and its careful application. This section, and the checklists and details included here, will facilitate the application of Benchmarking within your own organisation.

Use this section as a focusing tool individually, compare the results with colleagues or send them in for us to analyse.

1 WHAT NEEDS TO BE DONE?

Action	Purpose	Who should be responsible	Date to be completed

WHAT SHOULD BE DONE WHEN?

Month / Date / Activity	1	2	3	4	5	6	7	8	9	10	11	12	13	14	15	16	17	18	19	20	21

3 RELATIONSHIPS OF MISSION STATEMENT TO MEASURABLE CRITICAL SUCCESS FACTORS

Mission/Vision Statement

	Yes	No
Has this been derived from a Senior Management workshop?	☐	☐

	Yes	No
Has it been examined for completeness?	☐	☐

	Yes	No
Has it been communicated to all staff?	☐	☐

	Yes	No
Have Critical Success Factors been identified?	☐	☐

	Yes	No
Are these derived directly from the Mission Statement?	☐	☐

Critical Success Factors

Complete the following table, specifying your organisation's Critical Success Factors and their implementation:

Critical Success Factor (CSF)	Measurable?	Is a target set?	Is it realistic?	Who is responsible for achieving it?
1				
2				
3				
4				
5				
6				
7				
8				

4 TARGETS

Review and amend your organsations' Critical Success Factors. For each of your organisation's Critical Success Factors specify improvement targets to be reached after 6, 12, 24, 36 and 60 months, or other appropriate periods.

Critical Success Factor	6 months?	12 months?	24 months?	36 months?	60 months?
1					
2					
3					
4					
5					
6					
7					
8					

How do you select targets?_____

Are they achievable?_____

How do you know?_____

_____

Is there a better way?_____

5 CURRENT PERFORMANCE AND IMPROVEMENT ACTIVITY

Critical Success Factor	Current Level/ Performance	Improvement Action Plan	Who is Responsible
1			
2			
3			
4			
5			
6			
7			
8			

6 PROCESSES

	Yes	No
Have you defined your core business processes?	☐	☐

	Yes	No
Are all stages listed, together with inputs, outputs, process owners and measurement points?	☐	☐

What do you measure for each process?

Core Process	Stages	Measurement Points	Process Owner
1			
2			
3			
4			
5			
6			
7			

How do you set targets?_____

_____

_____

_____

7 USE OF MEASUREMENT AND MONITORING TOOLS

Tools	Areas being used	Areas could be applied to	Why is it not being applied?	How should we approach Implementation?
1 PDCA 7 Tools of Quality Control 2 Pareto charts 3 Cause and effect diagrams 4 Stratification 5 Check sheets 6 Histograms 7 Scatter diagrams 8 Control charts				
9 Run charts				
10 SPC				
11 Taguchi Methodology				
12 QFD				
13 Process Deployment Flow Charts				
14 Cost of Quality				
15 Critical Success Factors				
16 Benchmarking				
17				
18				
19				
20				

How does your organisation know what matters to the customer and their relative importance?

_____

How do you know your organisation's performance in terms of these wants, and how do they compare to those of your competitors?

_____

8 VOICE OF THE CUSTOMER

	Yes	No
Does your organisation listen to the 'Voice of the Customer'?	☐	☐

How is it obtained?_____

_____

How should it be obtained?_____

_____

Construct a 'House of Quality' for one of your organisation's products or services.

Step 2
<u>Enter here</u>
the operating
requirements to
help achieve
customer wants

Step 4
<u>Here</u> try to
benchmark
against your
competitors on
a 1–5 scale

Operating
requirements

Customer
requirements

1   2   3   4   5

Step 1
<u>Enter here</u>
What matters to the
customer and their
relative importance
1–5 (5 is most
important)

Step 3
<u>Enter in</u> body of table
the connections between
what matters to the
customer and business
processes

9 BENCHMARKING

What processes for making comparisons with other organisations do you have in place?

_____

_____

_____

How do you obtain relevant data?_____

_____

_____

Specify below possible measurements within your organisation that could be the basis for Benchmarking.

Measure	Current performance	Physical Limit (if applicable)	Competitors' Performance A	B	C	'World's Best Practice'	Target/ Date	How to Close the Gap
1								
2								
3								
4								
5								
6								
7								
8								
9								
10								

10 BENCHMARKING QUESTIONNAIRE 1

1 How do you define this process? Please describe it.

_____

_____

2 Do you consider this process to be a problem or concern in your company? If not today, was it a problem in the past?

_____

_____

3 What is the measure of quality for this process? What are the criteria that you use to define excellence in process performance? How do you measure the output quality of this process? How do you measure progress in quality improvement?

_____

_____

4 How do you consider cost and schedule in this process?

_____

_____

5 How much and what type of training do you provide for the various job categories of the process team?

_____

_____

6 What process improvements have given you the best return in performance improvements?

_____

_____

7 What company, excluding your own, do you believe is the best in performing this process?

_____

_____

10 BENCHMARKING QUESTIONNAIRE 2

1 How do you define this process? Please describe it.

_____

_____

2 Do you consider this process to be a problem or concern in your company? If not today, was it a problem in the past?

_____

_____

3 What is the measure of quality for this process? What are the criteria that you use to define excellence in process performance? How do you measure the output quality of this process? How do you measure progress in quality improvement?

_____

_____

4 How do you consider cost and schedule in this process?

_____

_____

5 How much and what type of training do you provide for the various job categories of the process team?

_____

_____

6 What process improvements have given you the best return in performance improvements?

_____

_____

7 What company, excluding your own, do you believe is the best in performing this process?

_____

_____

11 BENCHMARKING PARTNER ANALYSIS

Measure	Company Name			
Business size – sales revenue				
– number of Employees				
Ownership of business				
Industry focus				
Organisation structure				
Type of manufacturing				
Company culture: – formality				
– participation				
– communication				
– Company competencies				

12 BUSINESS PERFORMANCE COMPARISON

Measure	Company Name			
1 Return on net assets				
2 Market share				
3 Debt-equity ratio				
4 Inventory (% sales)				
5 Revenue per employee				
6 Manufacturing overhead				
7 Capital interest (% sales)				
8 R & D (% sales)				
9 R & D investment efficiency				
10 New-product cycle time				
11 Forecast cycle time				
12 Order turnaround time				
13 Material lead time				
14 Production cycle time				
15 Customer response time				
16 Customer complaints (% shipments)				
17 Field returns (% shipments)				
18 Warranty rate (% shipments)				
19 Parts returned to supplier				
20 First-pass yield				
21				
22				
23				

13 BENCHMARKING ACTION PLAN 1

Process_____ _____
Critical Sucess Criteria:_____ _____
Process Owner:_____ Date:_____

Summary of Study Results

Objective	Goals
	Short-term
Benchmark Company:_____ Date Observed:_____ Level:_____ Rate:_____	Long-term
Strategy (owner)	Targets and Milestones

14 BENCHMARKING ACTION PLAN 2

Process_____

_____

Critical Sucess Criteria:_____

_____

Process Owner:_____ Date:_____

Summary of Study Results

Objective	Goals
	Short-term
Benchmark	
Company:_____	
Date Observed:_____	Long-term
Level:_____ Rate:_____	
Strategy (owner)	Targets and Milestones

This section will be of relevance if you decide to copy these checklists to Services Ltd for analysis

---

Total number of employees_____

Number of sites and locations_____

Nature of Core Business_____

Turnover_____

Do you have, or are you applying
for BS 5750/ISO 9000?   ☐   ☐   ☐

                                      Have   Applying for   Do not
                                                         have

Is the organisation undertaking a TQM programme?   ☐   ☐

                                                               Yes   No

---

Details for Correspondence

Name_____   Post_____

Telephone No._____   Extension_____

Company_____

Address_____

_____

_____

Fax No._____

Return to: Services Ltd.
               Quality & Reliability House
               82 Trent Boulevard
               Nottingham NG2 5BL
               Telephone (0602) 455285, Fax (0602) 817137

WHAT TO DO NOW

Having completed the forms, the next steps for you or your organisation may already be clear to you and your colleagues. However, if after having completed the forms, you feel that you do have additional questions which have been raised by the forms but which cannot be answered by their completion, then please do not hesitate to contact us at:

Services Ltd
Quality & Reliability House
82 Trent Boulevard
West Bridgford
Nottingham NG2 5BL
Telephone 0602 455285
Fax 0602 817137

We are experienced consultants in the fields of Total Quality Management and Benchmarking. In addition to consulting, lecturing and running workshops/seminars on the subjects, we carry out Benchmarking Surveys which assess the potential for Benchmarking within organisations.

INDEX

Abbey National, 231–235
Action plan, 247
American Express 58
Awards
    Award for Excellence in
        Benchmarking, 186–194
    Benchmarking Research Prize, 185
    Benchmarking Study Prize, 186
    British Quality Award, 184
    Deming Award/Prize, 8, 160–164
    European Quality Award, 4, 8, 60,
        107, 167–183
    Malcolm Baldrige Quality
        Award 4, 8, 161, 164–166
    President's Award for Quality and
        Productivity Improvement 130
AT&T, 157

Bean L L 56
Benchmarking
    Benchmarking Boom, 2, 3, 244
    Benchmarking Code of Conduct,
        208–211
    Benchmarking in the Public Sector/
        Public Sector Benchmarking, 8,
        123–135
    Benchmarking Studies, 116–119
    Benchmarking Teams, 114–116,
        197–198
    Competitor Benchmarking, 69
    External Benchmarking, 110–122
    Functional Benchmarking, 69
    Generic Benchmarking, 70
    Internal Benchmarking, 69, 88–109
    Physical Benchmarking, 3, 15, 52
    Process Benchmarking, 213
    Product Benchmarking, 214–215
BOC Special Gases Ltd, 96–109,
    223–226
British Gas PLC, 237–243
BS 5750, 8–11
BS 6000, 35

Cabinet Office, 131
Camp, Robert, 55
Charter
    Charter Mark, 134
    Charter Standard, 134
    Citizens' Charter, 134
    Confederation of British Industry
        (CBI), 2, 244
Coopers & Lybrand, 2
Costs
    Appraisal Costs, 41
    External Failure Costs, 42
    Internal Failure Costs, 42
    Prevention Costs, 41
Creative Service Sector, 158
Critical Success Factors (CFS), 24–27,
    55, 129, 249
Customer, 21
    External Customer, 26
    Internal Customer, 22, 223
    Voice of the Customer, 142, 154, 254

Deming, Dr Edwards, 14, 33–37
Deming Cycle 35
Dodge, Harold E, 32

East Midlands Electricity, 125, 127
Electronic Business 200, 78
EN 29000, 9
European Assessment Model, 168
European Foundation of Quality
    Management (EFQM) 167
Engineering
    Japanese Simultaneous Engineering,
        137
    Simultaneous Engineering, 138–142

Federal Quality Institute (FQI), 130
Feigenbaum, Armand, 13, 40–42
Fisher, Sir R A, 47
Florida Power and Light (FPL), 58, 153,
    161
Fortune 5000, 78

Gurus
  Japanese Gurus, 33, 46–52
  Quality Gurus, 8, 33–52

Hewlett Packard, Bristol, 212–215
Hitachi, 40
Honda, 58, 83, 84, 139

IBM, 226–230
ICL, 215–220
Institute of Quality Assurance, 31
International Benchmarking
  Clearinghouse, 3, 110
Ishikawa, Dr K, 35, 42–46
ISO 9000, 8–11, 26–27

Japan, 14, 34, 35, 45
Japan's Top 50 Companies Turn in a
  Strong Performance, 78
Japanese
  Union of Japanese Scientists and
    Engineers (JUSE), 35, 36, 37, 38, 45
Job Competencies, 96–107
Juran, Dr Joseph, 37–39

Kanban, 52
Kodak, 70

Measurement, 16–21
Measures
  Process Measures, 133
  Product Measures, 133
  Satisfaction Measures, 133
Mission Statement, 20, 21, 22, 23, 25,
  249

Nasa, 130
NCR (Manufacturing) Ltd, 76–82
Nottingham Trent University, 125

Orthogonal Arrays, 48

Pareto
  Pareto Principle, 38
Philips, 70
Plan-Do-Check Action (PDCA) Cycle,
  35, 36
Poka-Yoke, 50, 51
Process(es), 25
  Business Processes, 24–27, 63

Internal Business Processes, 199
  Process Deployment Flow Chart, 26

Quality
  Company-wide Quality, 44–45
  Cost of Quality/Quality Costs, 38, 68,
    129
  House of Quality, 143–147
  Seven Tools of Quality Control, 43
  Statistical Quality Control, 31–32
  Total Quality Control, 40, 41
  Total Quality Management (TQM),
    4, 7, 13–28, 29, 33, 54, 59–61, 64, 65,
    94
  Total Quality Management in Public
    Administration (UK), 125–128
  Total Quality Management in Public
    Administration (US), 130–131
  Total Quality Management
    Programmes, 4, 94, 95
  Total Quality Management
    Organisation, 6, 28
  Quality Assurance, 17, 27, 62
  Quality Circle/Quality Control Circle,
    22, 45–46
  Quality Control/Control of Quality,
    16, 30, 39
  Quality Function Deployment
    (QFD), 138, 142–155
  Quality Loss Function, 49
  Quality Methods Association, 155
  Quality Planning, 39
  Quality System, 9, 41
  Zero Quality Control, 51

R&D, 136, 137, 155–157
Rover Group, 82–87, 221–223
Royal Mail, The, 127

Scientific Management, 30–31
Services Ltd, 262, 263
Shewhart, Dr Walter, 31, 32, 33, 35
Shingo Shigeo, 49–52
Single-Minute Exchange of Die
  (SMED), 51, 52
Stakeholder, 126, 127
Statistical Process Control (SPC),
  29
Statistical Quality Control (SQC),
  31–32

Steering Group, 20, 95, 129

Table of Tables, 153
Taguchi, Dr Genichi, 46–49
   Taguchi Methodology, 142
Taylor, F W, 30
Times 1000, 78
Toyota, 47, 50, 51, 52
Troubleshooting, 206–207

UK, 2, 244, 245

Variation
   Common Causes of, 32
   Special Causes of, 32

Whitney, E, 30

Xerox
   Fuji Xerox, 3
   Xerox, 55–61